THIS PLANNER BELONGS TO

_____

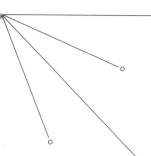

WEDDING
PLANNER

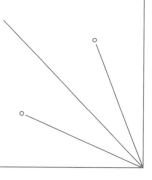

WEDDING PLANNER

KARA WEAVER

STERLING
New York

STERLING
New York

An Imprint of Sterling Publishing Co., Inc.
1166 Avenue of the Americas
New York, NY 10036

ISBN 978-1-4549-3573-5

Distributed in Canada by Sterling Publishing Co., Inc.
^{c}/o Canadian Manda Group, 664 Annette Street
Toronto, Ontario M6S 2C8, Canada
Distributed in the United Kingdom by GMC Distribution Services
Castle Place, 166 High Street, Lewes, East Sussex BN7 1XU, England
Distributed in Australia by NewSouth Books
University of New South Wales, Sydney, NSW 2052, Australia

For information about custom editions, special sales, and premium and
corporate purchases, please contact Sterling Special Sales at 800-805-5489
or specialsales@sterlingpublishing.com.

Manufactured in Malaysia

2 4 6 8 10 9 7 5 3 1

sterlingpublishing.com

Cover design by Igor Satanovsky
Interior design by Shannon Nicole Plunkett

CONTENTS

⚞ INTRODUCTION ⚟

Welcome to the adventure of engagement! An exciting time for both brides and grooms, the engagement period is a season of life that many don't forget quickly.

As you embark on this journey, don't forget the feeling of getting that ring on your finger, the excitement and nervousness of waiting to pop the question, and the tingling sensation you felt when you said, "YES!" Each and every part of your engagement story is special. Take a moment to reflect and write out your favorite part of your engagement story, or how you felt when you proposed. This can be a place for you to turn to when you are stressed or overwhelmed during your engagement season to remember the purpose of your marriage and why you want to share your wedding day with family and friends.

You can pass this down to your children and grandchildren one day as they embark on their own wedding planning journey!

_____

_____

_____

_____

_____

_____

This planner will allow you and your future spouse to journey through the process of engagement while maintaining your sanity and peace of mind. It provides a place to collect your thoughts, chart out different vendor options, and make the best decisions for you and your wedding day.

Throughout the planner you will find money saving tips, FAQs, planning charts, fun quizzes, and graphs to help guide you through your engagement.

The biggest thing for you to remember is that your wedding is YOUR day—it should represent you and your fiancé, not the expectations that others have for you. So take a deep breath, count to ten, flip the page, and LET'S DO THIS!

CHAPTER 1

So You Just Got Engaged . . . What Next?!

You've got your ring and your future spouse, and now all you need to do is plan a wedding! . . . Say what?

If only it were that simple.

Whether you've been wearing that shiny new ring on your finger for less than 24 hours or it's been a couple of months (or years) before you've made any official plans, it is finally your time to create the most perfect day for you and your boo.

Before you dive too deep into the world of wedding planning, you should know something very important: This time of life may be a stressful and pull-your-hair-out, anxiety-inducing season, but it is going to be amazing—repeat—everything is going to be *amazing*! Why? Because you have this handy-dandy bridal notebook that will become your best friend, your other lover, your . . . Maybe this is getting a little *too* carried away, but basically, this planner is your new best friend.

As you start planning, organizing, and creating, remember that you get to produce a day that is 100 percent about you and your boo, celebrating with your friends and family—now doesn't that sound fun?

Let's start with the basics. On the next page, talk with your future spouse and write out words that you both want used to describe your wedding.

Examples: "laid-back," "elegant," "farmhouse," "cozy," and so on.

Now that you know how you want your day to be described, take the quiz on the next pages to determine your overall wedding personality.

FOR THE BRIDE . . .

Who doesn't love a wedding personality quiz? Circle your style below (and get your boo to do the one on page 14 to compare results!)

1. I LIKE A RING THAT HAS A . . .

- **a.** Sparkling rose-gold halo
- **b.** Rough-cut crystal
- **c.** Vintage Art–Deco inspired cut
- **d.** Classic silver or platinum princess cut
- **e.** Simple gold circle cut

2. MY DREAM CEREMONY SITE IS A . . .

- **a.** Chic farmhouse
- **b.** Botanical garden
- **c.** Industrial loft
- **d.** Clean museum
- **e.** Intimate chapel

3. MY FAVORITE FLOWERS ARE . . .

- **a.** Delicate peonies
- **b.** Playful wild flowers
- **c.** Soft ranunculus
- **d.** White calla lilies
- **e.** Blushing roses

4. MY DRESS MUST BE . . .

- **a.** Delicate lace and tulle
- **b.** Off-the-shoulder and with appliqué
- **c.** Sentimental, with sparkles, and flirty
- **d.** Romantic, with a sweetheart neckline, and soft
- **e.** Crisp, satin, and classic

5. MY WEDDING DECOR WILL BE HEAVY WITH . . .

- **a.** Florals, crystal accents, and vineyard chairs
- **b.** Tapered candles, eclectic rugs, and family-style seating
- **c.** Antique china, feathers, and gold accent candles
- **d.** Satin table linens, pillar candles, and eucalyptus
- **e.** White satin table linens, mercury glass votives, and silver Chiavari chairs

6. MY BRIDESMAIDS WILL WEAR . . .

a. Varying shades of soft-colored chiffon

b. Mismatched easy-going, floral maxi dresses

c. Short, fun dresses that are perfect for dancing

d. Subdued neutrals and flowing fabrics

e. Matching off-white, floor-length gowns

7. MY SIGNATURE DRINK WILL BE . . .

a. Chilled Rosé

b. Margaritas

c. Champagne tower

d. Aperol spritzers

e. Craft beer and wine

8. WE WILL BE SERVING . . .

a. Light finger foods, chicken piccata, and macarons

b. Cheese boards, pasta bar, and donuts

c. Florentine biscuits and finger sandwiches edged with edible flowers

d. Four-course plated meal and classic wedding cake

e. Easy apps, chicken or beef options, and wedding cupcakes

9. MY BOO AND I WILL DRIVE AWAY IN A . . .

a. Glamorous white convertible

b. Flower-covered Volkswagen bug

c. Retro Rolls-Royce

d. Simple silver sports car

e. Sleek limo

10. WE'LL HONEYMOON IN . . .

a. Paris

b. Dubai

c. Italy

d. Greece

e. Hawaii

Mostly A's

WEDDING ROMANTIC

DESCRIPTION: You love a good rom-com, and rose gold is your aura color. You live on macarons, and if you could choose anywhere in the world for your honeymoon, you'd be jetting off to Paris faster than you can say "baguette."

WORDS AND COLORS TO DESCRIBE YOUR STYLE: Enchanting, rose petals, whimsical, nostalgic

BRIDES LIKE YOU: Cinderella & Kate Middleton

Mostly B's

WHIMSICAL BOHEMIAN

DESCRIPTION: Flower crowns, mismatched dresses, and dream catchers—oh my! This style embodies the free spirits of you and your boo, and you've been dreaming about your wildflower field ceremony since the day you were born.

WORDS AND COLORS TO DESCRIBE YOUR STYLE: Eclectic, boho chic, flower child, free-flowing fabrics

BRIDES LIKE YOU: Hayley Paige & Nikki Reed

Mostly C's
VINTAGE ENTHUSIAST

DESCRIPTION: The word *candelabra* makes your heart melt, and the idea of incorporating actual antiques in your table decor brings tears to your eyes.

WORDS AND COLORS TO DESCRIBE YOUR STYLE: Old World, wrought iron, historic, retro

BRIDES LIKE YOU: Audrey Hepburn & Kate Moss

Mostly D's
MODERN MINIMALIST

DESCRIPTION: You prefer an aesthetic that focuses on the people rather than the surroundings. You believe in a "less is more" mind-set and push to incorporate neutral tones into your wedding day.

WORDS AND COLORS TO DESCRIBE YOUR STYLE: Sleek, neutral undertones, blank-slate wedding venues

BRIDES LIKE YOU: Solange Knowles & Mila Kunis

Mostly E's
CLASSIC TRADITIONALIST

DESCRIPTION: You're basically a reincarnation of the Queen herself. You like timeless elegance, and no wishy-washy wedding trend is going to steer you away from your black-tie affair.

WORDS AND COLORS TO DESCRIBE YOUR STYLE: Elegant, classic, refined, black and white

BRIDES LIKE YOU: Grace Kelly & Beyoncé

FOR THE GROOM . . .

We know, we know—your fiancée made you take this *insert rolling eye emoji here*. We promise by the end of this quiz, you'll be asking your groomsmen to take it, too.

1. I PROPOSED AT . . .

a. A family outing

b. The location of our first date

c. The peak of our favorite hiking

trail

d. Our home with our pups

e. Against the city skyline

2. MY IDEAL BACHELOR PARTY INCLUDES . . .

a. A night at a secretive speakeasy

b. A nostalgic dinner with my guys

c. Did someone say "camping"?

d. Smoking cigars and drinking whiskey

e. An evening of poker, blackjack, and cards

3. MY GROOMSMEN AND I WILL WEAR . . .

a. Pin-striped suits and snazzy suspenders

b. Custom suits in colors to match the blushing bride

c. Casual khakis and a floral button-down collared shirt

d. Navy suit pants, a button-down collared shirt, and a tie

e. Classic black tie tux

4. MY SIGNATURE DRINK WILL BE . . .

a. Whiskey neat

b. Champagne

c. Mulled apple juice

d. Craft beer

e. Bourbon on the rocks

5. I WILL EAT...

a. Baked ham, mashed potatoes, and lemon cake

b. Stuffed chicken with a pesto drizzle and red velvet cake

c. A variety of international tapas and chocolate strawberries

d. Fajitas and tres leches cupcakes

e. Steak, green beans, and chocolate cake

6. I WILL REGISTER FOR A...

a. Record player

b. Bar cart

c. Portable hammock

d. Tool set

e. A grill utensil set

7. I WILL GIFT MY GUYS...

a. Personalized whiskey flasks

b. A picture from the bachelor party and some personalized socks

c. Natural, organic cologne

d. Personalized shot glasses and a bottle of their favorite liquor

e. Engraved pocketknives

8. MY IDEAL UNIQUE WEDDING VENDOR IS A...

a. Cigar maker

b. String quartet

c. Photo-booth alpacas

d. Classical guitarist

e. DJ and drummer mix combo

9. I'LL DRIVE OFF IN A...

a. 1920s Rolls-Royce

b. Limo

c. Vespa

d. Convertible

e. Range Rover

10. WE'LL HONEYMOON IN...

a. Cuba

b. Paris

c. Zion National Park

d. Cancún

e. Hawaii

Mostly A's

GATSBY GENTLEMAN

DESCRIPTION: The Great Gatsby has nothing on you! Add some vintage flair, a foxtrot, and cigars, and you are one happy man.

WORDS TO DESCRIBE YOUR STYLE: Old World, wrought iron, historic, retro

GROOMS LIKE YOU: Frank Sinatra & John F. Kennedy

Mostly B's

REGAL ROMANTIC

DESCRIPTION: You know your fiancée has a tendency to go for a dramatic flair, and you are all about it, too! Rose petals and candles don't sound too bad . . . as long as there are some chocolates and champagne for you both to enjoy as well.

WORDS TO DESCRIBE YOUR STYLE: Enchanting, rose petals, whimsical, nostalgic

GROOMS LIKE YOU: Prince Harry & Sterling Shepard

Mostly C's

BOHO BABE

DESCRIPTION: You have a free-spirited mind-set and are the adventurous one of your friends. Your closet has multiple suspender options, and if you could, you would wear bold-patterned button-downs and a man bun every single day.

WORDS TO DESCRIBE YOUR STYLE: Eclectic, boho chic, flower child, free-flowing fabrics

GROOMS LIKE YOU: Nick Jonas & Winston Marshall

Mostly D's

THE MINIMALIST MAN

DESCRIPTION: You would prefer saving your money for an amazing honeymoon rather than a large, over-the-top wedding. Your focus is on people, not your surroundings, so placing more emphasis on the ways people interact at your wedding is a priority.

WORDS TO DESCRIBE YOUR STYLE: Sleek, neutral undertones, blank-slate wedding venues

GROOMS LIKE YOU: Michael Phelps & Dax Shepard

Mostly E's

TACTFUL TRADITIONALIST

DESCRIPTION: You understand that marriage is more than just the wedding but also believe in having a little fun. You like following the rules and making a straightforward plan of action.

WORDS TO DESCRIBE YOUR STYLE: Elegant, classic, refined, black and white

GROOMS LIKE YOU: Kit Harrington & Prince William

ow that you know your wedding style, it's time to pick some key elements you can use when you scour the internet and bridal magazines. Choose between the words or items below that best describe your ideal wedding day, and see how well you and your boo match up. And don't worry if you have differing choices; the best weddings are blends of two styles!

FOR THE BRIDE . . .

1. White or ivory
2. Roses or greenery garlands
3. Veil or flower crown
4. Wedding train or short 'n' sweet
5. Tux or suspenders
6. Margaritas or champagne
7. Beer or whiskey
8. DJ or band
9. Candles or flowers
10. Outdoor or indoor ceremony
11. Buffet or sit-down meal
12. Taco bar or stuffed chicken
13. Brunch or evening reception
14. Bubbles or sparklers
15. Long or short bridesmaids' dresses

FOR THE GROOM . . .

1. White or ivory
2. Roses or greenery garlands
3. Veil or flower crown
4. Wedding train or short 'n' sweet
5. Tux or suspenders
6. Margaritas or champagne
7. Beer or whiskey
8. DJ or band
9. Candles or flowers
10. Outdoor or indoor ceremony
11. Buffet or sit-down meal
12. Taco bar or stuffed chicken
13. Brunch or evening reception
14. Bubbles or sparklers
15. Long or short bridesmaids' dresses

LET'S REFLECT:

What questions did you and your future spouse answer the same?

_____

_____

_____

_____

_____

_____

What questions did you and your future spouse answer differently?

_____

_____

_____

_____

_____

_____

Now that you have a general idea of the styles you like, think about how long an engagement you each want. Your wedding timeline will ultimately depend on the length of your engagement. To help you decide in which season to marry, take a peek at the pros and cons of each one.

SPRING

PROS

a. There are only limited major holidays at this time of year, which means that your guests don't have to worry about competing for travel days.
b. There are not as many weather-related restrictions when it comes to choosing your dress.
c. The majority of outdoor venues will have naturally beautiful scenarios to work with, helping you cut costs on decor.

CONS

a. Allergy season is in full force! Take note if you are planning on having both your ceremony and reception outdoors.
b. There is an increased demand for vendors and venues, so prices will be higher during this season.
c. If you have a quick engagement, it may be more difficult to book your top-choice vendors, as they may have already been reserved.

SUMMER

PROS

a. It's ideal for couples who want late-night weddings—you can plan for a ceremony that starts at 6:30 or 7 p.m.
b. There's the most amount of sunlight for your ceremony and reception.
c. Most of the flowers you want will be available. Summer has the largest number of choices for in-season flowers, so the majority of options will be available to you.

CONS

a. Summer sun can equal harsh lighting for photos.
b. The heat can be distracting for guests during your ceremony or outdoor reception.
c. The heat and humidity can affect your hair and makeup on the big day. Prepare to schedule touch-ups throughout your wedding day with your hair and makeup artist.

FALL

PROS

a. In hotter climates, the fall can be the best option for couples who want milder temperatures on their wedding day.

b. In the majority of climates, the chance of rain isn't high, so your outdoor wedding can be tent-free.

c. This season can require minimal decor, especially if your venue already includes gorgeous color-changing trees and foliage.

CONS

a. If you are a fan of the rustic-barn theme, these venues book up well over a year in advance, as the themes and style of fall make them desirable locations for weddings.

b. Dates book quickly during this season with vendors, too, so be sure to reserve your top vendor choices ASAP.

c. With summer vacations ending and the holidays right around the corner, the fall can be a financially tight time for people getting married, so budget accordingly.

WINTER

PROS

a. This is typically a slower season for vendors, which means you can save more.

b. If you are marrying in a church near the holidays, you can probably use their already set-up decor and save money on your ceremony site designs.

c. Snow photos! Need we say more?

CONS

a. The holidays may prevent many of your guests from coming.

b. There's a limited amount of daylight for your ceremony and photos.

c. Outdoor weddings are COLD! The weather can be a game changer, too, when it comes to snow, freezing temperatures, or storms.

After looking through the seasonal pros and cons, choose two times when you would be comfortable having your wedding. Then follow the steps on the next page to guarantee that your wedding date won't clash with current events, and hone in on a specific date for your big day!

TOP 5 TIPS

TO REMEMBER WHEN CHOOSING
A WEDDING DATE

1. Mark off important preexisting dates (graduations, holidays, family vacations/reunions, work trips, etc.) that could inhibit people from coming.

2. **$$$ Saving Tip:** Booking a wedding on a Sunday or Friday can help you save thousands of dollars, as these are less high-demand wedding dates for couples.

3. Aiming for a three-day weekend allows guests (and you!) to have an extra day to travel home (or for the honeymoon) without needing to take vacation time from work.

4. Think about where you want to honeymoon. Is it best to travel there right after your wedding, or is it better to honeymoon later, depending on the weather, hurricane season, and so on?

5. Decide if you want to get married indoors or outdoors, and what season is best for your decision. (If you need help, refer back to the pros and cons list for each season on pages 20–21.)

Who doesn't love a good mood board? Sketch out ideas here (and on the following two pages), use it as your note keeper, or cut out photos you love from wedding magazines and build your very own vision board.

Etiquette for the Modern Day Wedding Registry

The wedding registry concept didn't start until the 1920s, when Macy's department store created an opportunity for couples to request specific gifts from their wedding guests as they started their new life together. Fast-forward almost a hundred years, and the wedding registry has evolved quite a bit. Instead of registering for just china and silver, couples are now asking for cash and charitable donations.

So how do you put together a modern-day registry? Your registry is a guide guests can refer to so that they can know what items would best serve you and your future spouse once you're married. Keeping an updated, personalized registry ensures that you won't receive multiple plates of fine china but, instead, items that match your lifestyle and day-to-day activities. As you start thinking about the items for your registry, there are four rules of thumb you should consider:

1. Register for gifts in different price tiers.

  - Divide your registry by price. Items in the $25 to $100 range would be the lowest price tier, while those priced between $100 and $250 would be the middle tier, and $250 and up are high-end. Typically, you want 35 percent of your registry in the first tier, 45 percent in the second tier, and the remaining 20 percent in the third price tier.

2. Register at different stores.

  - With the price tier in mind, feel free to register at two or three stores (having four is too many, five would be overkill). These stores can vary in types of gifts—for example, Target versus Home Depot—but they should all contain the different-priced items discussed above.

3. Prioritize needs versus wants.

- While your boo may want the newest Xbox® or PS4™, neither may be the best thing to put on your wedding registry. Prioritize household items you may need, like sheets, towels, dishes, and home decor. You can also provide an option for guests to donate money toward gift cards for certain stores that you can use at a later date for your wants.

4. Consider where your gifts will be shipped.

- In the twenty-first century, you may find that the majority of your gifts will be bought online. With that in mind, make a decision as to where your gifts should be sent. This could be your current house, if you plan on staying there before and after the wedding, or it can be your in-laws' or parents' home. Make sure that the shipping address is a place you trust and where you know your gifts will be properly stored until you can get to them.

So How Do I Keep Track of My Wedding Registry Items?

Even knowing what to register for can be an extremely daunting task, but don't worry! Whether you're living together and have the majority of standard household items, or are moving in together for the first time, here's a list that will allow you to check off items that you may not have even thought about!

ITEM	STORE (REGISTERED AT)	ITEM	STORE (REGISTERED AT)
BLENDER		ELECTRIC SKILLET	
COFFEEMAKER (French Press, Espresso maker, or Instant coffee maker)		MICROWAVE	
		PANINI PRESS	
COFFEE GRINDER		DEEP FRYER	
TEA KETTLE		ICE CREAM MAKER	
JUICER		KNIFE SET	
FOOD PROCESSOR		STEAK KNIVES	
STAND MIXER		KNIFE SHARPENER	
HAND MIXER		SKILLETS	
SLOW COOKER		SAUCEPANS	
PRESSURE COOKER		LARGE COOKING POT	
TOASTER		CASSEROLE DISH	
TOASTER OVEN		CAST-IRON SKILLET	
WAFFLE IRON		POT RACK	

ITEM	STORE (REGISTERED AT)	ITEM	STORE (REGISTERED AT)
FONDUE POT		CAN OPENER	
BAKEWARE		GARLIC PRESS	
BAKING SHEETS		PIZZA WHEEL	
CAKE PANS		SLOTTED SPOON	
MUFFIN TINS		KITCHEN UTENSIL HOLDER	
COOLING RACKS		LADLES	
COOKIE CUTTERS		SALAD SPINNER	
TRIVETS		COLANDER	
MIXING BOWLS		CUTTING BOARDS	
ROLLING PIN		RICE MAKER	
CAKE DECORATING KIT		ICE CREAM SCOOP	
CAKE STAND		PEPPER MILL	
MEASURING SPOONS		KITCHEN TIMER	
MEASURING CUPS		BASTING BRUSH	
SPATULAS		PAPER TOWEL HOLDER	
WHISKS		SOAP DISPENSER	
TONGS		TRASH CAN	
CHEESE GRATER		APRONS	
CITRUS ZESTER		DISH TOWELS/CLOTHS	
VEGGIE PEELER			

ITEM	STORE (REGISTERED AT)	ITEM	STORE (REGISTERED AT)
DISH RACK		FLATWARE SET	
OVEN MITTS		BUTTER KNIFE	
POT HOLDERS		SALAD SERVERS	
CASUAL PLACE SETTINGS		SERVING FORKS	
DINNER PLATE SET (12)		WHITE WINE GLASSES	
BOWLS (12)		RED WINE GLASSES	
COFFEE MUGS		WATER GLASSES	
SALT & PEPPER SHAKERS		MARGARITA GLASSES	
SERVING PLATTERS		MARTINI GLASSES	
SUGAR BOWL & CREAMER		SHOT GLASSES	
SERVING BOWLS		JUICE GLASSES	
SALAD BOWL		BEER MUGS	
BUTTER DISH		WINE CHILLER	
CAKE PLATE		COCKTAIL SHAKER	
FORMAL DINING SET (This would be your "fancier" plates for special occasions, such as the holidays or dinner parties)		ICE BUCKET & TONGS	
		BAR TOOLS	
		COASTERS	
		CARAFE	
		TABLECLOTH	
TEAPOT & TEA CUPS		NAPKINS	

ITEM	STORE (REGISTERED AT)	ITEM	STORE (REGISTERED AT)
NAPKIN RINGS		LAUNDRY HAMPERS	
PLACEMATS		LAMPS	
FLAT & FITTED SHEETS		THROW PILLOWS & BLANKETS	
DUVET		CANDLES	
DOWN COMFORTER SET		FURNITURE	
BED SKIRT		ELECTRONICS	
MATTRESS PAD		WALL CLOCK	
BLANKETS		WALL MIRROR	
PILLOWS		DECORATIVE LIGHT FIXTURES	
PILLOWCASE SET			
PILLOW SHAMS		PATIO FURNITURE	
BATH TOWELS		PATIO UMBRELLA	
BATH SHEETS		BARBECUE SET	
HAND TOWELS		WHEELED COOLER	
WASHCLOTHS		GRILL	
GUEST TOWELS		LUGGAGE TAGS	
BATH MATS		LUGGAGE	
SHOWER CURTAINS		TRAVEL TOTES	
SCALE		CASH REGISTRY	

*K*eeping track of the whos, whats, whens, and wheres are crucial for organizing both your registry and thank-you list. It's recommended that you put all of your information in one place so you'll be able to track who gave you what, when they gave it to you, and when you wrote/sent a thank-you note.

ITEM RECEIVED	WHO GAVE IT

THANK YOU NOTES

WHEN IT WAS RECEIVED	WHERE IT WAS RECEIVED	THANK YOU WRITTEN?

Item Received	Who Gave It

When It Was Received	Where It Was Received	Thank You Written?

Item Received	Who Gave It

WHEN IT WAS RECEIVED	WHERE IT WAS RECEIVED	THANK YOU WRITTEN?

Item Received	Who Gave It

WHEN IT WAS RECEIVED	WHERE IT WAS RECEIVED	THANK YOU WRITTEN?

ITEM RECEIVED	WHO GAVE IT

When It Was Received	Where It Was Received	Thank You Written?

ITEM RECEIVED	WHO GAVE IT

WHEN IT WAS RECEIVED	WHERE IT WAS RECEIVED	THANK YOU WRITTEN?

You know you'll be scouring the never-ending layers of Pinterest, wedding websites, and blogs galore, so if you are forgetful and don't want to lose your vision boards, keep track of your user names and passwords for all of your wedding needs.

MONEY SAVING TIP: It is helpful to create a new email account solely for your wedding. You can keep track of vendor sales and specials and won't have to worry about getting bombarded with emails in your regular inbox after the wedding! You can close out the email accounts after your wedding.

USE THE CHART BELOW TO KEEP TRACK OF ALL OF YOUR
WEDDING WEBSITES AND LOGINS

WEDDING WEBSITE NAME	USERNAME	PASSWORD

CHAPTER 2

BUDGETING YOUR WEDDING &
PRIORITIZING YOUR NEEDS

The most important thing you can do as you prepare for your wedding day is to create a budget. No matter who is paying for your wedding, whether it is your parents, family members, friends, or you and your boo, having an idea of how much you are going to invest in your wedding day is a practice that can save you hundreds of dollars in the long run.

You should also consider the top three things you want to prioritize in your budget. Are there any nonnegotiables for your big day? Here are some of the most common ones:

- A live band instead of a DJ
- China plates instead of paper
- Marrying in a church versus a wedding venue
- A fully stocked, open bar instead of only beer and wine

You can refer to the quiz in chapter 1 for ideas about different wedding options. While all of these are wonderful features to include on your wedding day, the majority of time you will need to choose two or three nonnegotiables in order to stay within your budget. Both you and your future spouse should write out your individual nonnegotiables and compare them. If you have different opinions, take some time to talk through and find ways to compromise.

You've done all your pinning on Pinterest and wedding-photographer stalking on Instagram, now it's time to write out all of the things you want for your dream wedding.

Once you have charted them out, circle the top three items that are nonnegotiable for each of you.

THINGS I MUST HAVE	THINGS I HAVE NO PREFERENCE ON
Live 5-piece band	Having a buffet to save money on catering
Fajitas and Margaritas	Outdoor or indoor ceremony
Designer Dress	Kids at the reception

BRIDE'S LIST

THINGS I MUST HAVE	THINGS I HAVE NO PREFERENCE ON

EXAMPLE CHART FOR GROOM

Things I Must Have	Things I Have No Preference On
Whiskey	What kind of flowers we have
Good food	Photographer
Photo booth	Location of the wedding

GROOM'S LIST

Things I Must Have	Things I Have No Preference On

Wedding Cost Estimates

Your wedding vendors will vary in prices, but as you are building your budget, you should expect to spend the following amounts on each category. Here's a breakdown of expenses for the average wedding with a budget of $30,000.

WEDDING BUDGET — $30,000	INDUSTRY AVERAGE %
VENUE, FOOD & BEVERAGE	**40%**
VENUE (RECEPTION)	
CATERING/FOOD (INCLUDING FOOD, SERVICE, FLATWARE, STEMWARE, CHINA, ETC.)	
BARTENDING/BEVERAGE SERVICES	
DRINK COSTS	
CAKE/DESSERT (DON'T FORGET CUTTING FEES!)	
WEDDING INSURANCE	
SUBTOTAL	$12,000
CEREMONY SPECIFICS	**2%**
MARRIAGE LICENSE	
OFFICIANT	
CEREMONY MUSIC	
SUBTOTAL	$600
PHOTOGRAPHY/VIDEOGRAPHY	**9%**
PHOTOGRAPHER	
VIDEOGRAPHER	
PHOTO BOOTH	
SUBTOTAL	$2,700

DECOR	10%
FLOWERS (PERSONAL & DECOR FLOWERS)	
OTHER DECOR (CANDLES, GUESTBOOK, RING PILLOW, ETC.)	
LIGHTING	
RENTALS (LINENS)	
SUBTOTAL	$3,000

STATIONERY/PAPER GOODS	4%
SAVE THE DATES	
INVITATIONS (INCLUDING RSVP CARDS)	
OTHER (MENU, PROGRAM, ESCORT CARDS, ETC.)	
POSTAGE	
SUBTOTAL	$1,200

ATTIRE	8%
OUTFITS FOR BRIDE & GROOM	
ACCESSORIES/MISCELLANEOUS	
HAIR & MAKEUP COSTS	
ALTERATIONS	
SUBTOTAL	$2,400

ENTERTAINMENT	8%
DJ/BAND/ETC.	$2,400

PLANNER/COORDINATOR	10%
WEDDING PLANNER/COORDINATOR	$3,000

MISCELLANEOUS	5%
TRANSPORTATION, GIFTS, FAVORS, EXTRA FEES, ETC.	$1,500

EMERGENCY FUND	4%
ALWAYS SET ASIDE 4% TO 5% OF YOUR BUDGET, JUST IN CASE.	$1,200

GRAND TOTAL $30,000

Here's a blank template for you to use in creating your budget:

WEDDING BUDGET —

INDUSTRY AVERAGE %

VENUE, FOOD & BEVERAGE	40%
VENUE (RECEPTION)	
CATERING/FOOD (INCLUDING FOOD, SERVICE, FLATWARE, STEMWARE, CHINA, ETC.)	
BARTENDING/BEVERAGE SERVICES	
DRINK COSTS	
CAKE/DESSERT (DON'T FORGET CUTTING FEES!)	
WEDDING INSURANCE	
SUBTOTAL	

CEREMONY SPECIFICS	2%
MARRIAGE LICENSE	
OFFICIANT	
CEREMONY MUSIC	
SUBTOTAL	

PHOTOGRAPHY/VIDEOGRAPHY	9%
PHOTOGRAPHER	
VIDEOGRAPHER	
PHOTO BOOTH	
SUBTOTAL	

DECOR	10%
FLOWERS (PERSONAL & DECOR FLOWERS)	
OTHER DECOR (CANDLES, GUESTBOOK, RING PILLOW, ETC.)	
LIGHTING	
RENTALS (LINENS)	
SUBTOTAL	

STATIONERY/PAPER GOODS	4%
SAVE THE DATES	
INVITATIONS (INCLUDING RSVP CARDS)	
OTHER (MENU, PROGRAM, ESCORT CARDS, ETC.)	
POSTAGE	
SUBTOTAL	

ATTIRE	8%
OUTFITS FOR BRIDE & GROOM	
ACCESSORIES/MISCELLANEOUS	
HAIR & MAKEUP COSTS	
ALTERATIONS	
SUBTOTAL	

ENTERTAINMENT	8%
DJ/BAND/ETC.	

PLANNER/COORDINATOR	10%
WEDDING PLANNER/COORDINATOR	

MISCELLANEOUS	5%
TRANSPORTATION, GIFTS, FAVORS, EXTRA FEES, ETC.	

EMERGENCY FUND	4%
ALWAYS SET ASIDE 4% TO 5% OF YOUR BUDGET, JUST IN CASE.	

GRAND TOTAL

The Importance of Prioritizing Certain Wedding Vendors over Others

Remember that it's important to define your priorities because then you can look at your budget and see how your wants and needs fit. Don't really care about having fancy, gold-foil-stamped stationery? Then go with a budget option for your paper goods and spend that extra $500 on your dress!

As the bride and groom, it is important to come to a consensus about how you want to allocate your wedding budget. Don't stress over it though! You've got this wedding-planning thing in the bag; all you need to think about is how to make the day 100 percent you.

Refer back to pages 46–47, where you and your groom listed your individual priorities, wants, and needs. Review what you both think is extremely important to incorporate at your wedding, as well as other areas that may not be the most important for you both. Once you look that over, you will be able to create a budget that reflects your desires for your wedding day.

Wedding FAQs:

- HOW DO I CHOOSE HOW MANY PEOPLE I CAN AFFORD TO HAVE AT MY WEDDING?

- HOW DO I CREATE A GUEST LIST OF PEOPLE MY FUTURE SPOUSE & I ACTUALLY WANT?

Now let's talk about guests. Some bridal couples love creating their invite list, and others, well, they would rather dive into a pool of angry bees than figure out who to ask to their wedding day. Sound familiar?

All of your questions are soon to be answered. How many is too many? Do I really need to invite my crazy uncle Bill? And what about kids? What's the policy with them?

Here's the biggest reminder: your wedding is *your* day.

If there are people who make you uncomfortable or you honestly just don't want to have at your wedding, it's OK not to invite them. You are a strong, independent woman (and man!) who could very easily go to the courthouse and get married without anyone there, so it is a gift to your family and friends to witness your wedding ceremony. Don't be afraid to make your own choices and say no in order to make sure your wedding reflects your style and your theme.

Whether you want an intimate event or a lavish 500-person party, your wedding will be fun! There are things to consider though, as you plan for your ideal wedding guest count. . . .

4 Things to Consider
WHEN YOU CREATE YOUR GUEST LIST

1. **Decide on who is inviting whom.** If you have family helping you with the wedding, it is a good gesture to allow them a certain amount of invites for the wedding. These can be given to old family friends or relatives that your parents or in-laws may be close to, even if you are not. From there, decide how many spots you and your fiancé will allocate for friends, extended family, and coworkers.

2. **Cost.** The more people you invite, the more your wedding budget will increase. Feeding 100 people looks very different costwise than feeding 350 people. Make sure that your budget is able to accommodate large numbers of guests if you want to host a big gathering. Your per-guest cost will depend on the type of food and drinks you are serving, the location of your wedding, and the length of the reception. Refer back to your priorities and budget: if you want 300 people and have a $20,000 budget, you might need to refrain from having a full bar and opt for just beer and wine to help with costs!

3. **Your priorities.** Remember that activity on pages 46–47 where you wrote out your priorities for your wedding day? If "huge wedding guest count" wasn't listed, then put a foot on the brakes and say, "Whoa there, Nelly," because you may be biting off more than you can chew.

4. **Make rules (and stick to them!).** Sit down with your fiancé and write out some strict rules for your invitations. Not keen on kids? Then decide that no kids under the age of twelve will be invited. If you haven't spoken to a potential guest in over three years and they aren't a family member, then you can take them off your list. And if you're taking a guest off your in-laws' list, it would be a good idea, in good faith, to take a guest off your parents' list to keep things even.

While this process will seem difficult and tense at first, it will get easier! So take a deep breath and know that your invite list will be A-OK as long as you stick to your rules and remember your budget!

Below, write out some ideas for the guidelines you and your future spouse want to stick with when it comes to inviting guests. This way, you will be able to hold each other accountable.

1. _____

2. _____

3. _____

4. _____

5. _____

 GUEST COUNT PROS & CONS

0 TO 50 GUESTS

PROS

   a. This is best if you have a lower budget, or if you want a lavish event on a low budget, as you can spend more per person.

   b. You don't have to agonize over the guest list because you can keep it simple and intimate—no extended family, just Mom, Dad, and your closest friends!

CONS

   a. Some couples think small equals simple, but most of the time it doesn't. There are still many aspects of the wedding requiring wedding professionals that will eat at your budget.

   b. Having a smaller guest list may offend family and friends who didn't make the cut.

51 TO 100 GUESTS

PROS

   a. This gives you more venue options to choose from. There are so many beautiful sites out there, and many of them have limits as to how many guests can come. This guest-count range allows you the versatility of choosing a venue.

   b. You're more likely be able to tackle those DIY projects you've been eyeing on Pinterest! With a smaller number of wedding favors, table centerpieces, and crafts to create, you will have the time to invest in these projects without feeling overwhelmed.

CONS

   a. If you have a large family that you want to invite, they may take up the majority of your invite list.

   b. If your parents are paying for the wedding, it might be difficult to express to them that they can't invite everyone they want with a limited guest list.

101 TO 200 GUESTS

PROS

   a. This is considered the "sweet spot" for guest counts. The average wedding in the United States has 120 guests in attendance.

   b. This number of guests allows you time to mix and mingle with your guests without draining you and your groom. And it leaves time to still do all the fun things you want, like eat cake, dance, and spend some time with each guest throughout the night.

CONS

a. It can become more difficult to say hello to each of your wedding guests during the reception, as you will most likely not have enough time to have quality conversations with every individual.

b. Your costs per person start to add up quickly.

201 TO 300 GUESTS

PROS

a. Your wedding atmosphere is going to be off the charts! The more, the merrier, and you know your guests are going to love mingling, dancing, and meeting one another.

b. You get all the swag. A larger wedding typically means each guest will purchase more items from your registry.

CONS

a. Seating arrangements start to become difficult as you add more people and decide who is going to sit near or next to whom.

b. There are fewer venues to choose from, as many of them cap at 200 to 250 people. Be wary of venues that allow for larger guest counts but require you to pay a higher price.

300 PLUS

PROS

a. You can be more open regarding your guest list. Think about it—how often will all of your closest friends and family members be in one space to celebrate with you?!

b. You may receive discounted pricing from caterers, as they typically purchase in bulk, allowing you to take advantage of their lower costs per food items.

CONS

a. You may not be able to spend as much per person, pressuring you to cut out some aspects of your dream wedding to reallocate toward food and beverages.

b. Typically, there are more details, place settings, chairs, and tables that need to be arranged, adding stress to the couple and/or increasing the amount of time your planner will be designing and staging your reception and ceremony site.

$\mathcal{K}$ eeping track of your guest lists is ridiculous and time-consuming. You can use the template below to create an easy-to-use chart on your computer, or fill in the one in this book to track your wedding guests.

	LAST NAME	FIRST NAME	RSVP (YES OR NO)
1			
2			
3			
4			
5			
6			
7			
8			
9			
10			
11			
12			
13			
14			
15			
16			
17			
18			

Food Choice	Attending Rehearsal Dinner (yes or no)	Rehearsal Food Choice	Needs Hotel Room (yes or no)

	LAST NAME	FIRST NAME	RSVP (YES OR NO)
19			
20			
21			
22			
23			
24			
25			
26			
27			
28			
29			
30			
31			
32			
33			
34			
35			
36			
37			
38			

Food Choice	Attending Rehearsal Dinner (yes or no)	Rehearsal Food Choice	Needs Hotel Room (yes or no)

	LAST NAME	FIRST NAME	RSVP (YES OR NO)
39			
40			
41			
42			
43			
44			
45			
46			
47			
48			
49			
50			
51			
52			
53			
54			
55			
56			
57			
58			

Food Choice	Attending Rehearsal Dinner (yes or no)	Rehearsal Food Choice	Needs Hotel Room (yes or no)

	Last Name	First Name	RSVP (yes or no)
59			
60			
61			
62			
63			
64			
65			
66			
67			
68			
69			
70			
71			
72			
73			
74			
75			
76			
77			
78			

Food Choice	Attending Rehearsal Dinner (yes or no)	Rehearsal Food Choice	Needs Hotel Room (yes or no)

	LAST NAME	FIRST NAME	RSVP (YES OR NO)
79			
80			
81			
82			
83			
84			
85			
86			
87			
88			
89			
90			
91			
92			
93			
94			
95			
96			
97			
98			

Food Choice	Attending Rehearsal Dinner (yes or no)	Rehearsal Food Choice	Needs Hotel Room (yes or no)

	Last Name	First Name	RSVP (yes or no)
99			
100			
101			
102			
103			
104			
105			
106			
107			
108			
109			
110			
111			
112			
113			
114			
115			
116			
117			
118			

Food Choice	Attending Rehearsal Dinner (yes or no)	Rehearsal Food Choice	Needs Hotel Room (yes or no)

	LAST NAME	FIRST NAME	RSVP (YES OR NO)
119			
120			
121			
122			
123			
124			
125			
126			
127			
128			
129			
130			
131			
132			
133			
134			
135			
136			
137			
138			

Food Choice	Attending Rehearsal Dinner (YES OR NO)	Rehearsal Food Choice	Needs Hotel Room (YES OR NO)

	LAST NAME	FIRST NAME	RSVP (YES OR NO)
139			
140			
141			
142			
143			
144			
145			
146			
147			
148			
149			
150			
151			
152			
153			
154			
155			
156			
157			
158			

Food Choice	Attending Rehearsal Dinner (yes or no)	Rehearsal Food Choice	Needs Hotel Room (yes or no)

TALLY UP TOTALS IN EACH COLUMN:

Number of Guests Coming to Reception: _____

Guests Reception Food

    Choice 1: _____

    Choice 2: _____

    Choice 3: _____

Number of Guests Coming to Rehearsal Dinner: _____

Guest Rehearsal Food

    Choice 1: _____

    Choice 2: _____

    Choice 3: _____

Number of Guests That Need a Hotel Room: _____

Chapter 3

Planning Calendar: What to Do & When to Do It

Wedding timelines can be both a pain in the rear and the best thing you ever did for your engagement. Planning a wedding is way more stressful than trying to solve an escape room game, but the objections are pretty similar: finish the task at hand as fast as you can.

A wedding-planning timeline helps you chart out the short- and long-term goals for your wedding day. The best thing about wedding planners is that you already have one right in your hand! By looking through the suggested upcoming tasks per month, you can take a deep breath and remember that Rome wasn't built in a day, and it will take time to get everything in order for your wedding, too.

Depending on the length of your engagement, the planning process may be either longer or shorter than what is described here. Following are the most common tasks that come with planning a wedding. Take a look and add them to the calendar on the following pages to keep your deadlines at front of mind.

WEDDING CHECKLIST

As you start to plan your wedding, refer to the list of all the things that need to be done beforehand. While there are a lot of items to check off, it is important that you delegate tasks to different people, like your mom, maid of honor, wedding planner, and future spouse, to help create your perfect wedding day and release some stress off of your mind.

TASK	PERSON RESPONSIBLE
10 TO 12 MONTHS BEFORE THE WEDDING	
BOOK A WEDDING PLANNER OR WEDDING MANAGER!	
DECIDE ON CITY AND SEASON	
SAVE WEDDING DRESS PHOTOS	
START A FAVORITES BOARD (FLOWERS, DRESSES, DECOR, PICTURES, ETC.)	
SAVE FLOWER PHOTOS	
SAVE DECOR PHOTOS	
SAVE WEDDING CAKE/DESSERT PHOTOS	
SAVE MENSWEAR PHOTOS	
RESEARCH VENUES	
RESEARCH CATERERS & BAKERS	
RESEARCH FLORISTS	

TASK	PERSON RESPONSIBLE
RESEARCH WEDDING INVITATIONS	
RESEARCH DJS & CEREMONY MUSIC	
RESEARCH PHOTOGRAPHERS/VIDEOGRAPHERS	
DECIDE ON THEME & COLORS	
SCHEDULE ENGAGEMENT PHOTO SHOOT	
BUY DRESS	
BUY "SAVE THE DATES"	
BOOK CEREMONY & RECEPTION SITES	
BOOK OFFICIANT	
CREATE WEDDING WEBSITE	
SCHEDULE WEDDING DRESS FITTING APPOINTMENTS	

8 TO 9 MONTHS BEFORE THE WEDDING

CREATE GUEST LIST & ESTIMATE GUEST COUNT	
CREATE WEDDING BUDGET	
MEET WITH PHOTOGRAPHERS/VIDEOGRAPHERS	
SIGN UP FOR PREMARITAL COUNSELING	
MEET WITH FLORISTS	

TASK	PERSON RESPONSIBLE
SCHEDULE TASTINGS WITH CATERERS & BAKERS	
DECIDE ON HEADPIECE & VEIL	
DECIDE ON BRIDAL BOUQUET	
DECIDE ON BRIDESMAIDS' BOUQUETS	
DECIDE ON GROOMSMEN'S & GROOM BOUTONNIERES	
DECIDE ON ADDITIONAL CORSAGES, BOUTONNIERES, BOUQUETS	
BOOK DJ/ CREATE PLAYLIST FOR YOUR SPECIAL DANCES, CEREMONY, AND RECEPTION	

6 TO 7 MONTHS BEFORE THE WEDDING

TASK	PERSON RESPONSIBLE
BLOCK OUT HOTEL ROOMS FOR GUESTS	
BOOK WEDDING-NIGHT HOTEL	
BOOK PHOTOGRAPHER/VIDEOGRAPHER	
BOOK CATERER/BAKER	
RESEARCH DECORATION IDEAS	
BOOK BARTENDERS	
CREATE WEATHER PLAN B	
MAKE A BEAUTY PLAN	

TASK	**PERSON RESPONSIBLE**
REGISTER FOR GIFTS	
SEND "SAVE THE DATES"	
CREATE PROGRAMS & OTHER PAPER GOODS	
DESIGN AND CREATE INVITATIONS	
PLAN BACHELORETTE PARTY WITH BRIDESMAIDS	
PLAN REHEARSAL DINNER	
SAVE HAIR & MAKEUP PHOTOS	

4 TO 5 MONTHS BEFORE THE WEDDING

PLAN FOR RENTAL DECOR & SOLIDIFY DECOR IDEAS	
GET WEDDING INSURANCE	
BUY INVITATIONS	
ASK FLOWER GIRL & RING BEARER	
DECIDE ON FLOWER GIRL'S & RING BEARER'S OUTFITS	
DECIDE ON FLOWERS FOR FLOWER GIRL	
DECIDE ON SEATING ARRANGEMENTS FOR RECEPTION: FREE SEATING OR ARRANGED SEATING?	
BUY/RENT MENSWEAR	
BUY WEDDING BANDS	
BUY STAMPS FOR INVITES	

TASK	PERSON RESPONSIBLE
BUY SHOES FOR WEDDING DRESS	
MAIL WEDDING INVITES	
MAKE TRANSPORTATION PLAN FOR AFTER RECEPTION	
MEET WITH HAIRSTYLISTS	
LIST EXTRA ITEMS TO BUY (GARTER, RECEPTION GIFTS, THANK-YOU GIFTS, ETC.)	
BOOK FLORIST	
1 TO 3 MONTHS BEFORE THE WEDDING	
DECIDE ON FINAL CEREMONY & RECEPTION DECOR	
DECIDE ON REHEARSAL OUTFITS	
DECIDE ON SPEECH RESPONSIBILITIES	
BUY UNDER-THE-DRESS ESSENTIALS	
BUY WEDDING FAVORS	
BUY EXIT SPARKLERS	
BUY BRIDESMAIDS' & GROOMSMEN'S GIFTS	
BUY PARENT THANK-YOU GIFTS	
BOOK HAIR & NAIL APPOINTMENTS	
CREATE HONEYMOON PACKING LIST	
CREATE DAY-OF SCHEDULE WITH WEDDING PLANNER	

	TASK	PERSON RESPONSIBLE
	FOR PHOTOGRAPHER, CREATE LIST OF REQUESTED CEREMONY & RECEPTION PICTURES	
	CONFIRM PAYMENTS & ARRIVAL TIMES WITH VENDORS	
	HAVE HAIR & MAKEUP TRIAL	
	GET MARRIAGE LICENSE	
MONTH OF WEDDING		
	GET MARRIED	
	TURN IN MARRIAGE LICENSE	
	HAVE WEDDING DRESS CLEANED & PRESERVED	
MONTH AFTER WEDDING		
	FINISH THANK-YOU CARDS	
	CHANGE NAME	
	POST PHOTOS TO FACEBOOK & SHARE WITH FRIENDS	

Once you look at the tasks at hand and the general time when they should be completed, fill out the calendar on the next couple of pages to give yourself space to have deadlines for each project.

$\mathcal{M}$ONTH _____

Task	Appt./Due Date	Completed
Ex: Meet with the florist —		✓
	Saturday, Feb. 16th @ 1:30 p.m.	

MONTH _____

Task	Appt./Due Date	Completed
_____		☐
_____		☐
_____		☐
_____		☐
_____		☐
_____		☐
_____		☐
_____		☐
_____		☐

Task	Appt./Due Date	Completed
		☐
		☐
		☐
		☐
		☐
		☐
		☐
		☐
		☐

MONTH _____

Task	Appt./Due Date	Completed
		☐
		☐
		☐
		☐
		☐
		☐
		☐
		☐
		☐

MONTH _____

Task	Appt./Due Date	Completed
		☐
		☐
		☐
		☐
		☐
		☐
		☐
		☐
		☐

MONTH _____

Task	Appt./Due Date	Completed
		☐
		☐
		☐
		☐
		☐
		☐
		☐
		☐
		☐

CALENDAR

MONTH _____

Task	Appt./Due Date	Completed
_____		☐
_____		☐
_____		☐
_____		☐
_____		☐
_____		☐
_____		☐
_____		☐
_____		☐

MONTH _____

Task	Appt./Due Date	Completed
		☐
		☐
		☐
		☐
		☐
		☐
		☐
		☐
		☐

Task	Appt./Due Date	Completed
		☐
		☐
		☐
		☐
		☐
		☐
		☐
		☐
		☐

MONTH _____

Task	Appt./Due Date	Completed
		☐
		☐
		☐
		☐
		☐
		☐
		☐
		☐

CALENDAR

MONTH _____

Task	Appt./Due Date	Completed
		☐
		☐
		☐
		☐
		☐
		☐
		☐
		☐
		☐

Task	Appt./Due Date	Completed
_____		☐
_____		
_____		☐
_____		
_____		☐
_____		
_____		☐
_____		
_____		☐
_____		
_____		☐
_____		
_____		☐
_____		
_____		☐
_____		
_____		☐
_____		

CALENDAR

THE WHOS, WHATS & WHENS

OF PLANNING BRIDAL SHOWERS, YOUR BACHELORETTE/BACHELOR PARTY & WHEN TO CHOOSE YOUR BRIDESMAIDS/GROOMSMEN

As if wedding planning wasn't busy enough, there are also some fun events to take into consideration as you get closer and closer to your big day. Bridal showers, bachelorette and bachelor parties, and Bridesmaid-Groomsmen get-togethers are opportunities to hang out with family and friends while the anticipation for your wedding day builds. Also, you have a pretty fun reason to go to Vegas, Napa, or even Disney with some of your favorite gal pals.

So let's dive in and talk about how to choose your bridal party. . . .

A very common complaint that brides and grooms have is the frustration over choosing their bridal party. Because movies often stereotype the ideal bridal party as including the quiet friend, the party friend, the hometown best friend, the new sister/brother-in-law, and the new BFF who replaces someone and starts a whole string of d-r-a-m-a, it's hard to envision what the "right" kind of bridal party is. And while movies can make for some funny moments, no bride or groom actually wants their bridal party fighting and tearing each other apart.

HERE'S A THOUGHT: Choose the women and men who have positively impacted you to become the person your future spouse adores.

Your best friend who taught you about forgiveness and empathy has given you a gift unlike any china set or vacuum cleaner on your registry, so include her or him in your big day.

When you choose people who love you for you and who love your spouse-to-be, your wedding-planning season will be not only fun but a beautiful time of life to share with your closest friends and family.

⚜

Still having trouble? Take our Bridal Party or Nah? quiz to help you and your groom narrow down your prospects!

———— BRIDAL PARTY OR NAH? QUIZ ————

BRIDE

1. Are they related to you?   YES   NO

2. Have you been friends longer than five years?   YES   NO

3. Have they met your family?   YES   NO

4. Were you a bridesmaid in their wedding?   YES   NO

5. Would this person get along with the rest of the bridal party?   YES   NO

6. Is this person someone you trust?   YES   NO

7. Is this person a sibling of your fiancé?   YES   NO

8. Does being around them make you happy?   YES   NO

9. Do you trust this person's opinion in a dressing room?   YES   NO

GROOM

1. Are they related to you?   YES   NO

2. Have you been friends longer than five years?   YES   NO

3. Have they met your family?   YES   NO

4. Were you a groomsman in their wedding?   YES   NO

5. Would this person get along with the rest of the bridal party?   YES   NO

6. Is this person someone you trust?   YES   NO

7. Is this person a sibling of your fiancée?   YES   NO

8. Does being around them make you happy?   YES   NO

9. Do you trust this person's opinion in a dressing or fitting room?   YES   NO

Mostly YES's

Hooray! This person is a strong candidate to become part of your bridal party. Now the only thing you have to do is pop the question!

Mostly NO's

Hmmm . . . sounds like this person may be a bit trickier to place. How about you trust your gut and nix this one off your list?

Now that you have your bridal party chosen, it's time to ask them! If your budget has some wiggle room and you want to pop the question to your bridal party in a fun and unique way, give them a "Will You Be My Bridesmaid/Groomsman?" gift! Here are some ideas for those.

FOR THE GIRLS...

1. Champagne and personalized champagne flutes

2. DIY spa kit in a box

3. Jewelry

4. Personalized tote bags

5. Monogrammed T-shirts

FOR THE GUYS...

1. Whiskey with personalized flasks

2. Engraved pocketknives

3. Beer cooler cups

4. Personalized cufflinks

5. Barbecue grill set with engraved wooden case

How to Plan an Amazing Bachelorette or Bachelor Party

You have your group, they have their gifts, now it's time to party! Planning a bachelorette or bachelor trip can be as low-key or as high-intensity as you want. Decide with your fiancé if you want your bridal party to travel as a group for a large vacation, or if you prefer to spend time apart and chill with your own friends.

Traditionally, the maid of honor and best man take the reins in planning the bachelorette/bachelor getaway, so ask your bridal party if they are interested in having that option to plan for you. If you want to plan the event, you go girl! Just remember not to stretch yourself too thin and to take a moment to enjoy your upcoming vacation. Wedding planning is stressful, and you deserve a break.

Once you decide who is in charge of planning the event, start brainstorming destinations and events you would like to do. If your bridal party is strapped for cash, take into consideration local staycations. Remember, your bridal party is so excited for you, but if they are paying for their dresses, travel and lodging for the wedding day, hair and makeup, and more, costs do add up fast.

Here are ten popular bachelor and bachelorette destinations to get the ball rolling.

10 OF THE Best
BACHELOR AND BACHELORETTE DESTINATIONS

1. Las Vegas, Nevada

2. Cancún, Mexico

3. Atlantic City, New Jersey

4. Austin, Texas

5. Nashville, Tennessee

6. New Orleans, Louisiana

7. Miami, Florida

8. Napa, California

9. New York, New York

10. Chicago, Illinois

Whether you choose to go deep-sea fishing off the beach of Costa Rica or wine tasting in Sonoma, California, your bachelorette or bachelor weekend will be one for the books! Take the opportunity to destress, get a massage, and enjoy time with your besties. Read on for the best tips you can follow for an amazing bachelorette party.

ᎢIPS FOR AN ᴀMAZING
BACHELOR/BACHELORETTE PARTY

1. Make sure your party reflects you.

- No one likes going to a party meant for them that is completely the opposite of everything they like. If all of your friends love the beach, but you would rather spend a weekend getaway skiing, then let them know. Your party should be fun for everyone, but especially for you, so be open and communicate with your party host.

2. It's OK to have a staycation!

- If finances are stretched, you may not want to spend a lot on airfare, lodging, and adventures for your vacay—and that is A-OK! Find some local options in your city, like a new up-and-coming brewery, music festivals, hike and bike trails, or even an spa day in your city's most exclusive area to feel as bougie as possible.

3. Have fun.

- Your bachelor/bachelorette party is considered the last hoorah as an unmarried person, so have fun! Celebrate your upcoming wedding with your closest friends at your side. Reminisce about how gawky and awkward you may have been in middle school with your school friends, and joke with your sisters about how you tormented them when you were a kid. Enjoy your party!

BRIDAL SHOWERS

Your mom, aunt, grandma, and longtime family friends have probably asked you a million times by now about when they can plan a bridal shower for you. And you may be 100 times over it already or completely over the moon about the idea of another reason to celebrate your wedding day. Either way, it's important to remember these dos and don'ts for your wedding showers.

☑ **DO:** Keep your showers to a minimum. No, we're not talking about your personal hygiene, but suggesting that you keep your wedding showers to two or three total. If you have many people offering to host, ask them cohost so as not to tire you out, but also so you don't invite your wedding guests to multiple events before the wedding. Send the hosts your availability in advance so that they can plan ahead.

☒ **DON'T:** Invite people to multiple showers unless they are immediate family or your maid of honor. It is generally expected that the bridal shower guests bring gifts to each event (i.e., the shower and the wedding), so inviting them to multiple wedding showers can become excessive.

☑ **DO:** Give thank-yous to your hosts and hostesses for throwing the event for you. A small, personalized gift can go a long way to show your appreciation to the people who have taken time to invest in your upcoming marriage.

DON'T: Invite people who aren't invited to the wedding. This rule doesn't apply if, for instance, your office hosts a work bridal shower for you, or if you are having a small courthouse wedding.

DO: Have fun! Enjoy the experience of being "showered" with gifts by your close friends and family. This event gives you the time to speak one-on-one with family members and friends who you may not get to stop and talk with the day of the wedding, so soak up every second.

CHAPTER 4

CHOOSING YOUR VENDORS

Choosing the right venue is almost as stressful as choosing where you want to go out to eat—there are just so many amazing options! Between thinking about whether you and your boo want an outdoor ceremony or indoor reception, and whether you want a delicious "build your own" fajita bar or a s'mores station for the little ones you're inviting to your wedding, there can sometimes be too much information, leading to overload. And let's be honest, when you're overwhelmed with all the decisions and details, the last thing you want to do is think about anything wedding related.

While bridal expos, Facebook groups, and websites can be amazing resources for brides to learn about different vendor options, they can be slightly paralyzing, especially if you are starting with a blank slate and don't have a clear idea of what you want your wedding to look like. That's why it is so important to have the following section completed before you start talking with vendors.

When you have a solid vision, budget, and theme to work with, negotiating with vendors and knowing your limits will allow you to stay within your budget, while also checking off the top features you want for the big day.

MONEY SAVING TIP: It is extremely important to take notes while having consultations and exchanging emails with vendors, as it allows you both to be up-front and transparent about any rules, regulations, or issues that may pop up later and cause problems. And remember, it is YOUR day—not the vendors'! So don't bend if a vendor is pushing you to do something you are not comfortable with.

So how can you ensure that you are choosing the right vendors for your big day, as well as not spending an arm and a leg with them? Remember the activity that made you write out your top priorities for the wedding day? Look back at it! If you really want a live band over a DJ, make sure that you prioritize booking your favorite live music before spending all your budget on a dress and floral arrangements.

This section will give you questions to ask each vendor, charts to keep things organized, and a fun quiz to figure out if you should DIY or buy different décor items for your big day.

Your Vendors

There are so many vendor options to choose from for your wedding. While every wedding is different, it is important to have a solid understanding of who you can contract for your wedding, how much of your budget they typically take, and what kinds of questions to ask each vendor.

Your prices for each vendor will heavily depend on your theme, your style, and the size of your wedding. For weddings with more than 100 people, you can expect to spend more of your budget on vendors such as caterer, bartenders, linens, and decor, as you will have more tables to decorate in order to seat more people. For smaller, more intimate weddings, you can choose to devote less to the food and increase your spending for higher-end decor pieces, such as larger floral arrangements, large-scale backdrops for your ceremony site, or top-shelf liquor for your bar.

No matter what size wedding you have, these are the vendors that most weddings want or need.

1. **OFFICIANT:** The person who will be performing the wedding ceremony and signing your marriage license must be legally able to marry you in the state where your marriage license is submitted.

2. **VENUE/CEREMONY SITE:** These can be two different locations, but most wedding reception venues should also be able to provide a ceremony site on their property.

3. **TABLE AND CHAIR RENTALS:** The majority of wedding venues will be able to provide tables and chairs for your wedding; however, in the event they are not included in your property rental, you will need to contract with a chair and table rental company to provide seating during your ceremony and reception.

4. **CATERER:** This refers to the food provider for your cocktail hour and reception. It may also be your linen and staffing provider.

5. **LINEN PROVIDER:** This vendor is responsible for any tablecloths, napkins, and/or any other linens you need for your wedding.

6. **CUTLERY AND PLATE RENTALS:** These supplies are typically provided by your caterer; however, in the event that your caterer does not offer the plates you want for your big day, you will need to contract with a separate vendor to supply cutlery, dinner plates, cups, and napkins.

7. **STAFFING:** This includes the servers for your wedding. Most catering vendors can supply employees to assist with food service, cleanup, bussing, trash removal, cake cutting, and setting up your buffet lines. The type of staffing you need depends on the type of food you are serving.

8. **BARTENDING:** This is the staff that is certified to serve alcoholic beverages at your reception. The majority of venues will require proof of certification from these servers before the wedding day to ensure they are eligible to serve your guests.

9. **BAKER:** The dessert provider for your big day, they can be in charge of creating bridal cakes, groom's cakes, miscellaneous desserts, and setting up your cake table the day of the wedding.

10. **DJ/BAND:** The entertainment for the night, your DJ or band also typically assists with introductions, speeches, and cake-cutting and first-dance announcements.

11. **CEREMONY MUSICIANS:** These musicians provide instrumentals for your processional, ceremony, and recessional. These can also be supplied by a DJ, if you're opting out of live music during the ceremony.

12. **HAIR AND MAKEUP:** The vendors are in charge of giving you a glow-up on the day of your wedding. They may be two separate providers, or one stylist who can provide both hair and makeup services.

13. **PHOTOGRAPHER:** This vendor is in charge of capturing your wedding through a camera lens.

14. **PHOTO BOOTH:** This vendor supplies an interactive way to engage guests throughout the wedding reception. Your guests can pose for photos together—sometimes with props! Many couples opt to have the photo booth vendor have pictures printed for guests as a wedding favor from the event.

15. **VIDEOGRAPHER:** This vendor is in charge of capturing your wedding via video. This can be done through either a highlight film or a combination of documentary-style films.

16. **COORDINATOR/PLANNER:** The most integral part of your wedding day, this person is in charge of ensuring everything is running on schedule, vendors are on time, and your ceremony, cocktail hour, and reception run smoothly and efficiently. This is not the same person as a venue coordinator.

17. **VENUE COORDINATOR:** This person is in charge of the venue—not the bridal couple and the day's activities. The venue coordinator is the contact for the venue only and is not responsible for the wedding in any shape or form.

18. **LARGE RENTALS:** This vendor brings large-scale items, such as lounge areas, ceremony backdrops, and draping, to a venue.

19. **FLORIST:** This vendor purchases, arranges, and styles your bouquets, corsages, boutonnieres, tablescapes, and any other floral arrangements you want for your wedding.

20. **TRANSPORTATION:** This vendor can provide your getaway car, as well as shuttle buses for guests to use to and from the hotels where they are staying.

21. **HOTEL/LODGING:** These are the hotels or lodging options for your guests, bridal party, and family members to use during the days of your wedding.

Let's dive a little deeper into each type of vendor, and discuss price ranges and the best FAQs for each one.

VENUE/CEREMONY SITE

THINGS TO CONSIDER

When considering where you want to get married, here are a couple of questions to think about with your partner to ensure you are looking at and touring venues that will fit your style, theme, and budget. Start saving photos of your favorite venue pictures, and identify similar styles that pop up. Are you a fan of white walls and black iron beams on the ceiling? Or do you prefer an all-outdoor, tented option in a garden?

Venue shopping can get tricky, as each venue will have its own packages that vary in what is included. Some venues will include a specific amount of tables and chairs, while others will be as bare bones as possible, expecting you to rent tables and chairs at an additional cost. Certain venues may also have strict policies on the food and beverages that can be served, while others may have open-vendor policies for any wedding vendor.

To kick-start your venue vetting process, begin with these five questions to narrow down your venue style. Once you have a clear vision of your venue wants, reach out to five or six places that fit your style and budget and schedule on-site visits. Once you've had your tours, compare and contrast each venue's offerings by using the 49 Questions to Ask your Potential Venue on pages 110–117.

QUESTIONS TO ASK YOURSELVES
BEFORE YOU TOUR A VENUE

1. What is your maximum budget for a venue?

_____

2. Do you want to have a reception indoors or outdoors?

_____

3. Do you want an indoor ceremony option?

_____

4. Do you want to have your ceremony at a different location?

_____

5. What time of the year are you planning on getting married, and what does the weather typically look like during that time? (That is, if it's the rainy season or always over 100 degrees, getting married outside might not be your best option.)

_____

❧ 49 QUESTIONS ❧

TO ASK YOUR POTENTIAL VENDORS

	QUESTION	VENDOR 1 NAME:
1	WHAT DATES ARE AVAILABLE FOR MY WEDDING PREFERRED YEAR OR SEASON, AND WHAT PRICES DO YOU HAVE FOR SPECIFIC WEEKEND DAYS?	
2	FOR HOW LONG CAN THE VENUE BE RENTED FOR THE DAY?	
3	WHAT DOES THE RENTAL FEE INCLUDE?	
4	WHAT IS YOUR REQUIRED DEPOSIT?	
5	WHAT OUT OF MY PAYMENT IS REFUNDABLE? (I.E. SECURITY DEPOSIT, INSTALLMENTS)	
6	WHEN IS THE FULL PAYMENT DUE?	
7	DO YOU OFFER FLEXIBLE PAYMENT PLANS?	
8	HOW MANY EVENTS DO YOU BOOK ON A SINGLE DAY?	
9	DO WE NEED TO PROVIDE WEDDING PERMITS, INSURANCE, OR SOUND EQUIPMENT?	
10	WHAT IS EXCLUDED FROM THE RENTAL FEE?	
11	WHAT ARE THE SIZES AND NUMBER OF TABLES AND CHAIRS YOU HAVE? CAN YOU SHOW US A SAMPLE OF EACH TYPE OF CHAIR AND/OR TABLE?	
12	DO WE NEED TO MOVE CHAIRS FROM THE CEREMONY SITE TO THE RECEPTION SITE?	
13	DO YOU OFFER COCKTAIL TABLES FOR THE COCKTAIL HOUR?	

Vendor 2	Vendor 3	Vendor 4	Vendor 5
NAME:	NAME:	NAME:	NAME:

VENDORS

	QUESTION	VENDOR 1
		NAME:
14	ARE THERE POSSIBLE ADDITIONAL CHARGES BEFORE OR AFTER THE EVENT (FOR EXAMPLE, TAXES, ADDITIONAL SECURITY DEPOSIT, PARKING, SECURITY GUARDS FOR THE DAY OF THE EVENT)?	
15	IS THERE A SET-UP, BREAK-DOWN, AND/OR CLEANING FEE?	
16	WHAT DO WE NEED TO PICK UP/CLEAN/PACK OURSELVES?	
17	DO YOU HAVE A SPECIFIC TIME OUR EVENT MUST END?	
18	HOW MUCH SETTING UP DOES THE VENUE DO?	
19	IF THE NUMBER OF GUESTS CHANGES THE DAY OF OUR WEDDING, WILL THE VENUE PUT OUT AND REMOVE ADDITIONAL TABLES AND CHAIRS?	
20	ARE YOU HANDICAP ACCESSIBLE?	
21	WHAT IS YOUR POLICY WITH BARTENDING AND ALCOHOL?	
22	DO YOU PROVIDE TABLE LINENS? IF SO, HOW MUCH PER LINEN?	
23	HOW MANY BATHROOMS DO YOU HAVE, AND WHERE ARE THEY LOCATED?	
24	CAN YOU SHOW US YOUR BRIDAL AND GROOM SUITES, AND WHEN WILL THEY OPEN FOR OUR BRIDAL PARTY TO COME IN TO GET OUR HAIR AND MAKEUP STYLED?	
25	DO YOU ALLOW ANY VENDORS TO COME ONTO YOUR PROPERTY, OR DO YOU WORK WITH A PREFERRED VENDOR LIST?	
26	IF YOU HAVE A PREFERRED VENDOR LIST, DO YOU REQUIRE THAT WE BOOK ONLY WITH THOSE VENDORS?	
27	DO YOU HAVE ANY LIMITATIONS AS TO WHAT THE CATERER CAN DO ON-SITE (I.E., CAN A CATERER BRING BARBECUE SETUP, S'MORES BAR WITH AN OPEN FLAME, ETC.)?	

VENDOR 2	VENDOR 3	VENDOR 4	VENDOR 5
NAME:	NAME:	NAME:	NAME:

	QUESTION	VENDOR 1
		NAME:
28	WHAT IS INCLUDED IN YOUR KITCHEN FOR THE CATERER TO USE?	
29	WHAT IS YOUR POLICY FOR US VISITING THE VENUE SITE? DO WE NEED TO SCHEDULE AT A CERTAIN TIME IN ORDER TO ENSURE VENUE MANAGERS ARE ON SITE?	
30	WHAT IS THE SIZE OF YOUR RECEPTION HALL?	
31	HOW MANY PEOPLE CAN SIT IN THE RECEPTION HALL?	
32	DO YOU HAVE A RAIN-PLAN OPTION FOR AN OUTDOOR CEREMONY?	
33	WHAT IS THE SIZE OF YOUR CEREMONY SITE?	
34	DO YOU PROVIDE AN ON-SITE VENUE MANAGER THE DAY OF THE WEDDING?	
35	DO YOU RECOMMEND WE CONTRACT A WEDDING DAY COORDINATOR?	
36	WHAT IS THE DAMAGE DEPOSIT, AND WHAT IS THE POLICY TOWARDS GETTING IT RETURNED?	
37	WHAT SOUND AND LIGHTING EQUIPMENT DO YOU PROVIDE FOR THE CEREMONY/RECEPTION SITE?	
38	ARE THERE NOISE ORDINANCES WE SHOULD BE AWARE OF?	
39	DO YOU ALLOW US TO COME IN THE DAY BEFORE FOR THE REHEARSAL? IF NOT, CAN THE VENUE BE RENTED FOR A REHEARSAL AT AN ADDITIONAL COST?	
40	WHAT ARE THE CLOSEST OVERNIGHT ACCOMODATIONS?	
41	DO YOU ALLOW OPEN-FLAME CANDLES?	
42	CAN DRAPING BE HUNG FROM THE CEILING, OR DOES IT NEED TO STAND ALONE?	

VENDOR 2	VENDOR 3	VENDOR 4	VENDOR 5
NAME:	NAME:	NAME:	NAME:

QUESTION	VENDOR 1
	NAME:
43 WHAT ARE YOUR DECORATING LIMITATIONS?	
44 ARE THERE ANY RESTRICTIONS ON MATERIALS THAT CAN/ CANNOT BE USED FOR THE CEREMONY AISLE (E.G., FLOWER PETALS FOR THE FLOWER GIRL, ETC.)?	
45 CAN WE PROVIDE A DESIRED FLOOR PLAN? DO YOU HAVE TEMPLATES THAT WE CAN WRITE OUR DESIRED FLOOR PLAN OUT ON?	
46 DO YOU HAVE ANY RESTRICTIONS ON WHAT CAN BE USED FOR A GRAND EXIT?	
47 DO YOU ALLOW FIREWORKS?	
48 FOR THE CEREMONY, WHAT IS THE BEST TIME OF DAY FOR LIGHTING PURPOSES?	
49 DO YOU WORK WITH ANY HOTELS TO CREATE SHUTTLE SERVICES BETWEEN THE VENUE AND LOCAL HOTELS?	

NOTES:

_____

_____

_____

_____

_____

VENDOR 2	VENDOR 3	VENDOR 4	VENDOR 5
NAME:	NAME:	NAME:	NAME:

NOTES:

_____

_____

_____

_____

_____

_____

THE OFFICIANT

While the bride and groom are the showstopping main characters of the ceremony, your officiant sets the tone for guests before you walk down the aisle, so it is very important that you choose someone who can speak comfortably in front of a crowd and help you get rid of those wedding day jitters that will be with you at the altar.

There are so many options when it comes to choosing the officiant for your wedding day. Just as each couple is different, each wedding ceremony is as unique as a thumbprint. When it comes to booking an officiant, the most important part to remember is to keep it legal! Make sure your officiant—whether a family member, friend, pastor, rabbi, judge, or minister—is certified to marry you in the county and state where you are having your ceremony.

Online ministries can give your family member or friend a quick-and-easy way to become certified and perform the ceremony for you. Some websites require written applications with candidate's intentions for obtaining the certification, while others have simpler paperwork to fill out.

The ordainment process depends on the type of organization your officiant chooses to go through. It is strongly recommended that your officiant be certified sooner rather than later.

Your officiant is in charge of making sure that the ceremony itself runs smoothly. From the invitational to the vows, you should work with your officiant to craft a ceremony that is 100 percent you! Your officiant's biggest responsibility is the actual marriage license. Every marriage license is different in terms of which signatures it needs, so make sure to check with your county clerk and get all the required signatures before mailing it off. Your county clerk can also let you know how quickly the license must be turned in after the wedding.

MONEY SAVING TIP: Many states and county clerks strongly suggest that couples attend a premarital counseling workshop or classes to give them an opportunity to meet with their officiant before the wedding day. And many county and state clerks offer significant discounts in the cost of a marriage license if you take a premarital course and obtain proof of completion. Otherwise, you can expect a marriage license fee between $5 and $120, depending on your city, county, state, and residential status.

THE FLORIST

THINGS TO CONSIDER

Flowers are one of the most magical touches you can add to your wedding style. Your bouquet, boutonnieres, corsages, table arrangements, and ceremony's altar flowers can all be taken care of by a traditional florist. Many brides think that they can do all of the arrangements themselves, but they typically underestimate the time and care it takes to order, prep, and store the arrangements until the big day.

The best way to ensure that your floral design dreams are all coming true is by talking with your florist and having some sample photos of designs that you like. When you chat with your florist here are some other things to consider and discuss:

1. Have a list of your favorite flowers and ask what will be in season and what will cost extra if they are out of season.

   • Depending on the types of flowers, your wedding location, and the floral providers that your florist uses, some flowers may or may not be available at the time of your wedding. A great florist will be able to supplement your floral choices with similar flowers and make suggestions on how to mix seasonal florals with your must-have splurge items so you can stay within your budget.

2. Reuse floral arrangements created for the ceremony at your reception.

   • Use your arrangements for more than just one setting! This is especially true if you want large arrangements used at the altar and the head table of your reception. A wedding coordinator can make this switch for you on the wedding day. Additionally, many brides opt to have their bridesmaid's bouquets double as table centerpieces after the ceremony.

3. Look for full volume flowers.

- The larger the bloom, the fewer you need. By choosing large-petaled flowers (think sunflowers, Juliet roses, hydrangeas, etc.), your florist will be able to take up more space in the arrangements, meaning less cost for more space!

4. Fewer flowers, more greenery!

- A cost-effective way to keep your arrangements full is by adding greenery to each one. Eucalyptus, boxwood, and Italian ruscus are gorgeous ways to add a little oomph to your bouquets without breaking the bank. This also allows you to keep your flower numbers low, thus leading to a lower overall florist cost.

5. Pair your floral arrangements with other decor items.

- Adding supplements to your table decor, such as lanterns, candles, votives, picture frames, and gorgeous plates, cutlery, and cups, will have guests saying "wow!" to your tablescapes while keeping your floral budget from going over the top. Less is more when it comes to your flowers, and by pairing them with other items, you can create personalized and unique pairings for your table.

6. Buy wholesale, pay for the labor.

- Some florists offer brides the option of purchasing the flowers they want at wholesale prices from different shops, then delivering them to the florist to style and arrange. This helps brides find the best prices at different locations, and saves the florist time from sourcing the flowers on their own. Ask if your florist allows you to bring her the flowers you want so you don't get up charged for the extra time that goes into sourcing them.

7. Donate your florals after your wedding!

- A great way to get the most out of your floral budget is by donating your arrangements to different nonprofits, hospitals, nursing homes, or group homes for special needs adults and children. Many places will give you a tax deduction for your donations, so you are able to both brighten someone's day and get a tax break! Ask a family member, friend, or wedding planner to collect your arrangements after the wedding is over to take to a special location.

8. Create gifts!

- Another way to save money in the long run is by preserving some petals or a couple arrangements as gifts for your bridesmaids. For example, you can dry the petals of the bouquets and put them in clear Christmas ornaments as a wedding keepsake!

It is vital that you have a clear idea of how many and what kinds of arrangements you will need for your wedding. Below is a chart to help you keep everything in one place!

FLOWER ITEMS	# PER UNIT	FLOWER TYPE/COLORS YOU WANT	# OF STEMS NEEDED PER UNIT	TOTAL # OF STEMS NEEDED
Bride's Bouquet	1			

HOW LARGE WOULD YOU LIKE THIS ARRANGEMENT TO BE?

Bridesmaids' Bouquets				

HOW LARGE WOULD YOU LIKE THIS ARRANGEMENT TO BE?

Flower Girl's Crown				

HOW LARGE WOULD YOU LIKE THIS ARRANGEMENT TO BE?

Groom's Boutonniere	1			

HOW LARGE WOULD YOU LIKE THIS ARRANGEMENT TO BE?

Groomsmen's Boutonnieres				

HOW LARGE WOULD YOU LIKE THIS ARRANGEMENT TO BE?

VENDORS

Flower Items	# Per Unit	Flower Type/Colors You Want	# of Stems Needed Per Unit	Total # of Stems Needed
Ring Bearer's Boutonniere				

HOW LARGE WOULD YOU LIKE THIS ARRANGEMENT TO BE?

Altar Piece				

HOW LONG WOULD YOU LIKE THIS TO BE?

Table Decor				

HOW LARGE WOULD YOU LIKE THIS/THESE ARRANGEMENT(S) TO BE?

Pews/Seating				

HOW LARGE WOULD YOU LIKE THIS/THESE ARRANGEMENT(S) TO BE?

Cake Topper				

HOW LARGE WOULD YOU LIKE THIS TO BE?

CATERER

THINGS TO CONSIDER

When choosing a caterer, you need to figure out the best type of food service, food theme, and amounts for your wedding day. Some caterers also offer so much more than just food (think bartending options, table linens, cutlery, china plates and glasses, staffing options, etc.), so while you may spend more than anticipated on your caterer, you can get a lot of bang for your buck if they offer additional services.

Following are the types of offerings caterers typically provide, as well as questions to ask your potential vendor.

BUFFET: This is the most cost-effective option for couples looking to keep their food spending low. Guests are expected to grab their own plates and serve themselves during the reception. While buffet options are great for couples trying to keep their costs low, one thing to consider is that guests often have seconds or thirds, or self-serve more food than they actually eat, which could double (or triple) your overall expected catering costs. One way to prevent this is by having servers at your buffet who portion out meat options and sides for guests, keeping the amount of food consistent for everyone and eliminating any unexpected outages of food!

FAMILY STYLE: A happy medium for many couples is family-style plating. This allows the waitstaff to come to each table with large platters of food and people at the table then serve themselves—think Thanksgiving-table style. This is a very inviting and less formal way to keep guests at their tables during the reception, eliminating long lines

VENDORS

at a buffet station. This is also a strategic way of keeping your table decor items at a minimum, as the plates of food will be stored on the table until the meal is finished, and you want to make sure guests have adequate room to eat and pass plates without knocking over their water and wine glasses! This option does require more waitstaff than a buffet option, but less than a traditional plated meal.

TRADITIONAL PLATED: This option keeps guests at their tables while servers bring out the meal one course at a time. It is often considered a likely option for weddings that lean more toward a formal, black-tie atmosphere. This is the most expensive option for catering, as it requires the most staff to service your guests. Typically you are looking to staff one or two servers per table to keep your guests satisfied and full throughout the evening.

QUESTIONS TO ASK YOUR CATERER

1. Am I allowed to change the number of plates needed in case the final guest count is higher or lower than originally contracted? What is the additional cost to change that?

2. Do you assist with the cake cutting and plating for the event?

3. Do you offer place settings, silverware, and glasses? If so, how much do they cost in addition to the food?

4. Do you have a purchase minimum?

STAFFING SERVICE

THINGS TO CONSIDER

Most caterers will offer the option to book staffers with your food service. This allows the catering company to have quality control over the way their food is plated and served. If your caterer has an option to add on staffers to your service, it is best to use them as your first choice, as it allows for your caterer and staffers to remain consistent and prepare far in advance of your wedding date for floor plans, serving plans, and timing of clean up.

In the event that your caterer does not offer a waitstaff, it is highly recommended to bring in a third-party staffing service to assist with bussing tables, serving food, cutting the cake, and ensuring your venue is left clean at the end of the night. Many venues will hold your security deposit if you leave your venue in disarray.

A staffing company generally will not touch or clean personal items, so you should discuss with your planner or bridal party as to how the bridal rooms will be cleaned up at the end of the night, with bridesmaids taking their personal items and having your staffing company clean up trash and leftover food and beverages that are left in the room—you want to make sure you get that security deposit back, you budget-savvy bride!

BARTENDERS

Most caterers and staffing services will be able to provide bartenders for your event who are certified. The majority of venues do require that these servers are licensed and certified in your state, so if you end up getting free services from friends or family members, they must understand that they are still vendors who need to present certification to the venue in order to serve.

Fun options for bartenders are to have kegs, wine, and signature batch drinks for them to prep before your wedding so that they are able to serve your guests quickly. Try some of these popular signature drinks.

1. **MARGARITA:** Who doesn't love a little bit of tequila, lime, and salt? Add a punch to this drink by adding jalapeño juice or slices, or switch up the traditional lime flavor with strawberry, mango, or peach!

2. **MOSCOW MULE:** An easy drink to create in batches, the Moscow Mule offers an elegant twist to your bar setting. If there's room in your budget, have these drinks served in nonplastic cups so your guests can take insta-worthy photos of their drinks!

3. **SANGRIA:** You can make this classic drink fit any time of year! To best adhere to your wedding style, look for seasonal fruits that you can add to this perfect wedding drink.

BAKER

THINGS TO CONSIDER

No matter whether you want a five-tier wedding cake or a huge spread of various desserts, make your dessert options fun for your guests! If you have a traditional family recipe, ask your baker if they can re-create your grandmother's famous chocolate chip cookies for a sentimental addition to your table that your guests can enjoy, or ask your baker to design a cake that represents you and your soon-to-be spouse.

Many bakers can add personal aspects to your cake, so tell them that story of how you and your boo met while you were chowing down on *tres leches* cake with your girlfriends! Whether or not your guests know the stories behind the flavors, you will! And honestly, isn't that all that actually matters?

Following is a standard cake sizing chart. Depending on the number of people attending, you can opt to have a smaller bridal cake and cupcakes for guests to enjoy, or a large wedding cake that will be served to your entire guest list. Whatever you decide, make sure that you let your planner and baker know if you want to save the top tier for your one-year anniversary!

SERVING GUIDE

Wedding Cake Pieces
(1" x 2")

18	6"	6"	10
32	8"	8"	28
50	10"	10"	42
72	12"	12"	56
98	14"	14"	82
128	16"	16"	100

RENTALS

This aspect of wedding planning can be tricky. Revert to the DIY or Buy Quiz, below, to help you decide what you should be renting, buying, or DIYing yourself.

At the very least you will need tables and chairs where guests can sit and convene. Make sure you check with your venue to see if they supply these necessities, and if not, find a rental company that can deliver, set up, and pick up your large rental items, as well as smaller items like cutlery, plates, chargers, napkins, vases, candles, and so on.

If you start early enough, small items like signs, vases, and name cards can be made at home or bought from dollar stores, craft stores, or online marketplaces. Depending on your theme, style, and budget, you can decide whether you would prefer for a company to supply these items or if you would like to bring them yourself.

DIY OR BUY QUIZ

RULES: Count up the yes's and no's you have at the end of this quiz to determine if your idea is DIY-worthy or more easily bought or rented. Remember, the purpose of doing it yourself is to help cut costs and save you from stressing out, so if you are crafting any aspect of your wedding, plan accordingly and in advance! DIY items shouldn't be checked off at the last minute!

	YES	NO
1. Is this something I currently own that just requires being moved from one place to another?	☐	☐
2. Do I currently possess the skills to complete this task— that is, "I'm a graphic designer and know how to curate programs, signs, and invitations."	☐	☐
3. Can I prep and complete this project at least 30 days before my wedding so I am not working on it right before the wedding?	☐	☐
4. Are there people in my circle of influence who would be willing to help me complete this task?	☐	☐
5. Will this task save me more than $250?	☐	☐

TOTAL

Mostly YES's

You go, you craft queen! You have the artistic abilities of Pablo Picasso and the vision of Frida Kahlo.

Mostly NO's

Whoa, Nellie. While this seems like a good idea, it may be more of a hassle to craft rather than just taking a hit on the budget. Save your time and energy to devote to other things. Let this DIY project go, and move on.

DJ/BAND

Your emcee for the night and dance-floor-hype man/woman will be part of the band or the DJ who you book for your wedding. It is important that this vendor knows how to control and pump up a crowd, so ask for videos from past weddings, look over reviews from previous clients, and ask your potential vendors about their experiences.

Your DJ or lead band member will be in close communication with your wedding planner to ensure that they have a complete and updated schedule of events. They should know when to get the dance floor moving and when to quiet it down for events like speeches, first dances, and the cake cutting.

Most DJs ask for a list of requested songs, while bands will have you browse their lists of already rehearsed songs. In the event you want a specific song that is not in the band's repertoire, you may incur an additional cost, as the band members will need to schedule time to rehearse and learn your requested songs.

HAIR AND MAKEUP

If you currently have a hair stylist or salon that you go to, it is highly rec-ommended that you ask if they provide wedding-day styling for clientele. If they do, it is a fantastic investment on your end, as the hair stylist has experience working with your hair, which allows you to feel more at ease. If they do not provide makeup services, beauty professionals typically have contacts who they work with regularly who can come in on your wedding day to assist.

Try having one or two trial runs with your hair and makeup artists before your wedding day. Your hair and makeup artists (typically referred to as HMUA in the wedding world) come on the morning of your wed-ding to primp and prep you before you get into your dress. To make the most of your trials, try scheduling them the same day as your bridal photo shoot, so you and the artists have a clear idea of how long the process will take on your wedding day, and to give you both more confidence that your final look will be exactly as you envisioned!

VENDORS

WEDDING MANAGER/PLANNER

The most important thing you can do to ensure a stress-free day is not to believe the myth that "My site comes with a coordinator already, so I don't need a wedding planner!"

While having a venue on-site coordinator is helpful—they can get you extra trash cans for your reception and show you how to dim the lights in the reception hall—their main priority is keeping the venue in tip-top shape, not making sure the bride and groom are feeling 100 percent on their wedding day.

On the other hand, a wedding manager, most commonly referred to as "wedding coordinator," is the liaison between you and all of the other vendors you have hired for the big day, including the venue.

From confirming arrival and departure times, staying mindful of remaining balances and tips that need to be paid, and creating a schedule for the night to ensure activities are moving swiftly and according to plan, a wedding manager is there to be your No. 1 cheerleader, administrator, guide, and counselor throughout the day. Basically, they aren't there for just the day; they help plan and ensure that you are having a stress-free day.

When you book with a venue that comes with a venue coordinator, ask these five questions to better understand how your on-site venue employee will be helping *you*.

QUESTIONS TO ASK YOUR WEDDING PLANNER

1. Do you confirm with my vendors before the wedding day to ensure when they will arrive and depart, what services they are providing, and how much to tip/pay them?

2. Will you help to create a schedule for the wedding day and make sure that we are staying on it throughout the night?

3. If a vendor doesn't show up or is running late, how do you handle communicating and solving that with me?

4. Tell me how you help with setup and teardown on the day of the wedding.

5. Do you recommend that we use a day-of coordinator to help with the flow of events?

PHOTOGRAPHER

THINGS TO CONSIDER

The best advice when it comes to booking a photographer is to find someone who makes you feel 100 percent natural in front of the camera. No one likes faux, fake-looking photos, so ensuring that you and your photographer are compatible is the smartest thing you can do to make sure your photos represent you!

Check out wedding photographers on social media and review their online portfolios. Consider what kinds of filters you like and don't like. And think about how you look at your parents' photos and squeal and cringe at the same time because the photos seem so dated. To help make your final wedding photographer decision, consider the editing style of your photographer, and ask yourself whether it's trendy or classic.

VIDEOGRAPHER

As with your wedding photographer, hiring a wedding videographer who you feel comfortable with is going to make your wedding video so much more special. Make sure you have looked at potential vendors' past portfolio work, and find videos you like.

Your videographer can use the same editing style or storyboard for your video and add personal touches, like interviews with family members, recordings of reading your vows to one another, and incorporating your favorite songs to make your video more meaningful.

Ask your videographer about pricing options for filming your ceremony, along with, a 5- to 7-minute highlight film, and 30- to 45-minute documentary film. While you may not be able to add all of those in your package, you can pick and choose your top items and prioritize your videographer needs.

PHOTO BOOTH

THINGS TO CONSIDER

A fun option for favors is a photo booth that is available so guests can take photos and have a printed keepsake from your wedding day.

The type of photo booth you book can vary: some vendors offer unique background settings, like having the photo booth in an Airstream trailer, or the classic, customizable backdrop for you and your guests to use throughout the night, in which you can typically adapt the background, props, and photo prints to match your theme and wedding style.

MISCELLANEOUS VENDORS

THINGS TO CONSIDER

Couples can also decide to have unique vendor options to customize their wedding day. From table magicians to surprise live-music performances, you can create a day that is as unique to you and your spouse as you would like.

This is an opportunity for you to get creative, brainstorm some fun things that you both like, and then hop online for some inspiration on how other couples have incorporated these ideas into their own wedding day! Talk with your planner about past events he or she has worked and any creative ideas they may have to enhance and personalize your wedding!

Keeping Track of Your Vendors

Below is an area for you to keep track of all of your vendors, their contact information, and when they expect to be paid.

Vendor Type	Vendor Contact Name	Vendor Company
COORDINATOR		
BAKER		
CATERER		
DJ/BAND		
OFFICIANT		
BARTENDING		
STAFFING SERVICE		
PHOTO BOOTH		
FLORIST		
PHOTOGRAPHER		
VIDEOGRAPHER		
VENUE		
CEREMONY MUSICIANS		
OTHER		

Vendor Phone	Vendor Email	Payment Due	Paid In Full

CHAPTER 5

THE INS & OUTS OF THE CEREMONY

The excitement is building as you get ready with your pals and start counting down the hours (not days or weeks or months anymore!) in the final stretch. It is finally your wedding day, and you are about to start taking the literal steps toward marriage as your ceremony begins. But there's a whole lot that needs to happen before then if you want the day to run smoothly.

Let's take a second to rewind and get back to the beginnings of engagement. Professionals (and your bank account) highly recommend that you and your boo sign up for a premarital course before the wedding day. Why? Well, first off, taking a premarital course allows you and your future spouse to discuss topics that come into play while you are married. Issues like how to handle conflict or how you plan on managing your finances are important priorities that you can discuss in a healthy environment with a priest, counselor, or certified premarital coach.

Now, as for your bank account, did you know by taking a premarital course you can save between $50 and $100 on your marriage license? A little extra savings here and there can go a long way. As long as you have proof of completion, many agencies that issue wedding licenses will discount your license payment.

Check with your local town office, city hall, or courthouse to learn how to obtain a marriage license. Many places require, at the bare minimum, that both the bride and groom be present with valid, government-issued identification. You can email or call your local state office or state government websites to see if other paperwork, like birth certificates, divorce decrees, or blood tests, is required for your marriage license.

PREMARITAL COUNSELING OPTIONS

You can also check with your county clerk, courthouse employee, or state office to see what premarital counseling is available in your area and considered valid to receive a license discount. Many Catholic and Protestant churches offer options for couples getting married and are state certified as well. These are some of the issues that you may want to discuss in your premarital sessions:

- The number of children you both want (if any)
- Your relationship with money and how you plan on managing it
- How often you would like to see each other's in-laws
- Holiday planning and balancing extended families
- Religious upbringing and how you want to raise a family
- Where you would like to live (house, apartment, different city, etc.)

Premarital counseling is a fantastic opportunity to learn more about your future spouse and build a strong foundation as you enter into marriage.

FINDING AN OFFICIANT FOR YOUR WEDDING

You may be asking yourself, "I want my best friend [or family member] to officiate. How do they get certified?"

Finding an officiant is an important part of your engagement season. You can choose to have a priest, rabbi, nondenominational pastor, judge, or family friend officiate your wedding—as long as that person is certified and allowed to marry people in your county.

To become certified, your family member or friend can use organizations like the Universal Life Church, Church of Spiritual Humanism, or Church of Latter Day Dudes (spurred from the movie *The Big Lebowski*) via a quick Google search.

If you prefer to go with a traditional judge, religious leader, or clergyman, it is recommended that you reach out to them early in advance to confirm what they require in order to perform a wedding. Sometimes, officiants recommend that couples complete premarital training, which you can review on page 141.

Talk with your officiant about requirements and work with them to create a wedding ceremony that represents the love that you and your future spouse share.

To Write or Not to Write ... Your Vows

A GUIDE ON DECIDING WHAT TO INCLUDE

Speaking of your ceremony, let's talk about your vows! Some officiants will allow for the bride and groom to exchange personal, handwritten vows while others opt for a more traditional ceremony.

If you are looking to write your own vows, take a deep breath and relax. While expressing your love for someone in a short speech seems like a daunting task, I promise that your betrothed understands that your love can't be expressed in just a page of writing, but you can get close!

Following are sections where you and your boo can practice writing your vows to one another. Take time to write from the heart. Make a list of the top ten things you love about your significant other, or reminisce about the first time you realized you were in love. Either way, your vows are going to be something you will remember forever, so make sure you're being genuine and yourself.

BRIDE

_____

_____

_____

_____

_____

_____

_____

_____

_____

_____

_____

_____

_____

_____

_____

_____

_____

_____

_____

_____

GROOM

Choosing a Ceremony Location & Creating a Weather-Related Plan B

No one likes talking about it, but having a plan B is vital to ensuring that your wedding day runs smoothly in the event of inclement weather.

Talk with your wedding planner or venue to see what options they already have available for your wedding day. Typically, venues have an indoor ceremony area that you can use if necessary.

If your venue does not have the option to use a chapel or covered portico for your ceremony, you can opt to have a "hold" with a tenting company by paying a refundable deposit; this allows the tenting company to come out on short notice in case the weather changes abruptly.

You can also decide to have your ceremony in the same place as your reception. If you do opt to have this, you will need to consider what is called the "flip"—which means that your staffing company will take tear down the ceremony site after the ceremony and set up your tables and chairs for your reception while your guests are outside or at a different location for the cocktail hour. Make sure you communicate with your caterer and staffing service to do this for you right after the ceremony.

DIFFERENT TRADITIONS FOR WEDDING CEREMONIES

Every ceremony is different, from Catholic church ceremonies to small civil unions at the courthouse to eloping in Vegas. Your ceremony is an opportunity to include many different aspects of various traditions! Below are some examples to consider

- SAND POURING CEREMONY: This is also referred to as the "blending of the sands." Couples pour two different colors of sand together to create a multilayered vase of sand that represents two people coming together as a family.

- FIRST FIGHT BOX: You and your groom fill a box with a bottle of wine and love letters that you have written to each other and seal it during the wedding ceremony. The intention is to open the box after your first fight as a married couple, reading your letters and drinking the bottle of wine together to kiss and make up!

- UNITY CANDLE: The bride and groom both light individual candles and use those flames to light a third candle together to signify two people becoming one family.

SONGS YOU WANT PLAYED AT YOUR CEREMONY

Don't forget about your music! Setting the scene for your ceremony processional and recessional can be fun, traditional, sentimental, or a straight jam. Here are some popular tunes to get your brain started when choosing the best music for your processional and recessional.

FOR YOUR PROCESSIONAL . . .

1. "All You Need Is Love," The Beatles

2. "Perfect," The Piano Guys

3. "A Thousand Years," Christina Perri

4. "The Prayer," Josh Groban

5. "Canon in D," Johann Pachelbel

FOR YOUR RECESSIONAL . . .

1. "Don't Stop Believing," Journey

2. "Best Day of My Life," Imagine Dragons

3. "You Make My Dreams," Hall & Oates

4. "Dog Days Are Over," Florence and the Machine

5. "Here Comes the Sun," The Beatles

Ceremony Chart Schedule

To ensure your ceremony runs smoothly, have a clear outline of whom you want to walk down the aisle at what point and to what song. Use the chart below to help organize your thoughts!

FOR THE PROCESSIONAL . . .

ROLE	NAME (FEMALE)	ACCOMPANIED BY (MALE)	SONG
GRANDPARENTS OF BRIDE SET 1			
GRANDPARENTS OF BRIDE SET 2			
GRANDPARENTS OF GROOM SET 1			
GRANDPARENTS OF GROOM SET 2			
MOTHER & FATHER OF THE GROOM			
MOTHER OF THE BRIDE & USHER			
HOUSE PARTY & USHER			
HOUSE PARTY & USHER			

Role	Name (Female)	Accompanied By (Male)	Song
HOUSE PARTY & USHER			
HOUSE PARTY & USHER			
OFFICIANT			
GROOM			
GROOMSMAN & BRIDESMAID			
GROOMSMAN & BRIDESMAID			
GROOMSMAN & BRIDESMAID			
GROOMSMAN & BRIDESMAID			
GROOMSMAN & BRIDESMAID			
BEST MAN & MAID OF HONOR			
RING BEARER & FLOWER GIRL			
BRIDE & FATHER OF THE BRIDE			

FOR THE RECESSIONAL . . .

Role	Name	Accompanied By	Song Name
BRIDE & GROOM			
BEST MAN & MAID OF HONOR			
GROOMSMAN & BRIDESMAID			
GROOMSMAN & BRIDESMAID			
GROOMSMAN & BRIDESMAID			
GROOMSMAN & BRIDESMAID			
GROOMSMAN & BRIDESMAID			

CHAPTER 6

WHAT TO INCLUDE (OR NOT) IN YOUR RECEPTION

The reception occurs after the ceremony and traditionally includes a cocktail hour beforehand for guests to mingle, eat appetizers, and—surprise—drink cocktails, while the bride and groom have their photos taken as a couple and with their bridal party and families.

After the cocktail hour, guests are escorted into the reception hall to sit at their tables and await the announcement of the bride and groom.

Based on your personal preferences, the reception can include a meal for guests, dancing, and/or fun activities like a photo booth, lawn games, or opportunities to say hello to the bride and groom.

The top things to consider when creating your reception vision, timeline, and expectations are that it should be an enjoyable experience for you, your new spouse, and your guests. Take into consideration how long guests will be sitting at their tables, where they will be sitting, what kind of music will be playing, and when food will be served.

For your reception, you should talk with your wedding planner about how to bridge all of your ideas into one cohesive timeline. Remember, while it is 100 percent your wedding day, your wedding vendors have hundreds of hours' worth of wedding experience and want to ensure that your day is running smoothly, so ask them for recommendations!

WEDDING FAQ:

– HOW LONG SHOULD MY RECEPTION LAST?

Many brides make the mistake of having a very long, drawn-out reception. While it seems like a wonderful idea to spend seven hours dancing, by the end of the night, the majority of your guests will most likely have gone home, leaving your wedding send-off smaller than you may have wanted for photos.

The average wedding reception (including cocktail hour) lasts for four to four and a half hours and can include the following:

Cocktail Hour: 45 to 60 minutes

Receiving Line or Grand Entrance: 5 to 20 minutes

First Dance: 3 to 5 minutes

Toasts and Speeches: 15 to 25 minutes

Dinner: 45 to 90 minutes

Father/Daughter and Mother/Son Dances: 5 to 10 minutes

Open Dancing: 60 to 90 minutes

Wedding Cake Cutting: 5 minutes

Grand Exit: 5 minutes

COCKTAIL HOUR

The cocktail hour is a transition between the ceremony and reception. This section of your wedding day allows guests to mingle with one another, relax, grab a drink or two, and choose some small appetizers while the bride and groom take their remaining photos with friends and family. The length of the cocktail hour depends on how many photos your photographer needs to capture before the reception. Typically, the cocktail hour can last between 45 and 60 minutes.

RECEIVING LINE OR GRAND ENTRANCE

Depending on your preference, you may want to greet your guests as they move from the cocktail hour into your reception hall. Some couples ask their parents to join in on this, as many guests are friends and family members who want to say hello to everyone.

The entire bridal party or just the bridal couple can make the grand entrance. This allows your emcee or DJ to mention the names of your bridesmaids and groomsmen and introduces the newlyweds for the first time to their wedding guests. Typically, this grand entrance leads into the first dance.

FIRST DANCE

Often occurring right after the grand entrance, the newlyweds go to the dance floor and share their first dance together. If you are having a full seated, plated dinner, this can also happen right after the first salad course. If you and your spouse both have two left feet, opt for dance lessons ahead of your wedding day to practice. These are some popular dance options for couples:

1. TEXAS TWO-STEP: This dance is a popular tradition in the South and typically performed with a country or folk song.

2. WALTZ: Fitting a traditional-style wedding, this type of dance is paired with a mid-tempo ballad and will require lessons with a professional dancing coach if you don't already know how to waltz.

3. SALSA: A more up-tempo option for bridal couples, incorporating a salsa can be an amazing way for couples to honor cultural traditions and let loose during their first dance.

4. FOXTROT: This type of dancing can play to the strengths of your wedding dress if you want to "wow" guests with playful dance moves and twists. Consider taking a dance lesson or two in order to master this fun dance.

5. SWING: If you have a flair for vintage details, then swing dance is a perfect way to set the stage for your dance floor! Remember, with swing you want a lot of movement, so you both may want to make a quick change into something that allows you to move around.

6. FREEFORM: If you and your boo are already fantastic dancers and feel comfortable winging it the night of your wedding, then choose a song that means a lot to you both and dance your hearts out together!

7. FLASH MOB/CHOREOGRAPHED DANCE: Here's a fun way to energize your guests and possibly surprise them. You can work with a dance instructor to help create a wedding flash mob with your bridal party to entertain guests right at the start of the reception.

TOASTS

Toasts can happen right before the main course is served or just as guests are finishing their main course. Typically, the best man and maid of honor give toasts, followed by the parents of the bride or groom. Finally, the bride and groom can offer a thank-you message to their guests.

If your toastmasters are nervous about their upcoming speeches, have them follow this recipe for a memorable toast that will leave your guests laughing, crying, and clapping by the end.

Recipe for a Successful Toast:
The average toast lasts for 3 to 5 minutes, so practice saying your toast out loud to time it.

1. Introduce who you are and how you are related to the bride/groom.

2. Recollect a lighthearted memory of you and the bride/groom: a story of how you met or a funny memory you have that is *slightly* embarrassing (and that you have received approval from the bride/groom to share!).

3. Highlight something you admire about the bride/groom. This can be their ability to talk to strangers wherever they are, how they can make the most delicious chocolate chip cookies, or how they are always supportive of their friends and family.

4. Describe the moment when you heard the bride/groom talk about how they knew they had found "the one."

5. Wish them well for their future together and raise a glass to congratulate the newlyweds!

DINNER

Depending on when you want to have toasts, dinner will be served right before or after toasts are given. If you are having a buffet, guests can be dismissed by table either by your wedding planner or the DJ to go to the buffet line and self serve their food. If you have family style or plated seated dinner, your servers will bring out the food for guests to enjoy.

SPECIAL DANCES

Since you have already had your first dance, the mother/son and father/daughter dances can begin. Another popular option is for the bride and groom to have grandparents, uncles, aunts, or other people who have had a significant impact on their lives step in to dance with them. You can also take lessons for these dances and use the suggestions on page 161 to choose what kind of dance you would like to do.

OPEN DANCING

Now is the time to let your guests party! After your special dances, your DJ can announce that the dance floor is open, allowing your bridal party, family members, and other guests to get their groove on!

WEDDING CAKE CUTTING

This part of the night signals to guests that the party will be wrapping up within the next 60 to 90 minutes, so don't cut it too early! Typically, the cake is served with coffee. Make sure that your caterer or staffing service stays until then to help cut and serve the cake.

GRAND EXIT

At the end of the night, guests can send you off with well wishes and a grand exit. During this, guests can use glow sticks, sparklers, bubbles, rice, or flower petals (depending on your venue's item restrictions) for gorgeous photos!

SOME THINGS TO CONSIDER: if guests are throwing materials as you exit, some of them may get caught in your dress! If you would prefer to not to have birdseed stuck between your dress and your skin during the car ride to the hotel, you may want to stick with glow sticks or bubbles as exit materials.

ASSIGNED SEATING OPTIONS

No matter what kind of meal you plan on serving, it is highly recommended to assign table numbers for your guests.

No guest wants to make the mistake of sitting in a place where they shouldn't, so it is imperative that you reserve specific tables for immediate family, your bridal party, and your guests.

You can assign specific seats for guests, or, if you prefer guests to choose where they would like to sit at the tables, you can assign a specific number of people to a specific table, allowing them to choose which chair they want. This is the best option for couples who have chosen to go the family-style or buffet service route.

If you are opting in for a seated, plated meal, chair assignments are recommended for guests; you can give that information to your waitstaff so that they serve everyone according to their RSVP food preferences.

You will also need either to set up an extra table at the reception or have a couple empty seats throughout the reception hall for guests who did not RSVP or were somehow missed in the assigned-seating process. Make sure your caterer brings extra food to prepare in this instance, as it is best to make sure you have a spot for these guests.

Ask your wedding planner to assist you with seating assignments and make sure that your caterer and wedding planner both have copies of the assigned seating on the wedding day. This way, you won't be approached by guests or family members asking where they can sit.

You can have table numbers with signs that include the guests' names to guide them to their spots, and you can also showcase the assigned seating preferences during cocktail hour on a large sign or with escort cards.

Below are illustrations of how you would set up either situation.

Assigned Seat: _____

Assigned Table:

How to Serve Your Food

Look back at pages 125–126 where the differences between buffet, family style, and plated meals are discussed. Once you have decided on the eating arrangement and have booked it with your caterer, you can begin thinking about how you will lay out your reception hall either for guests to be served or to serve themselves.

BUFFET: No matter your wedding guest count, you will need at least two 8-foot tables to accommodate your buffet line. Try to place these tables toward the venue's prep kitchen area so your caterers don't have to move between tables and chairs to refill the chafing dishes.

BUFFET WITH CARVING STATION: You will need two 8-foot tables and, possibly, smaller tables at the end for your catering staff to use as carving stations. For this setup, try to incorporate two buffet lines and two carving stations to help guests get their food quickly and efficiently.

FAMILY STYLE: This serving style allows for your catering staff to bring food out to your guests that they will self-serve at the table. Note that when you use family style, you will need to have room on your tables for the excess serving dishes, so don't overload with decor!

SEATED, PLATED: Servers will need adequate room to move in between tables to get food to your guests quickly, so keep a walking path between all of your tables and chairs when you design your set-up area.

Use the following page to sketch out the layout of your venue!

Types of Plating for Your Guests

No matter your catering preferences, your tables will need to be set with plates, silverware, glasses, and napkins.

Remember, the more you add to your table for the place settings, the less you will need to invest in table centerpieces. You don't want to clutter your tables and make guests feel like they will knock glasses over or stick their elbows in the food!

Even if you are on a budget, setting the tables, instead of having guests grab plates at a buffet line, can enhance your tablescapes and add a personalized touch to the wedding experience. Acrylic plates are a fantastic option for brides on a budget who still want a more elegant dining option for their guests.

Wrapping silverware or using cloth napkins with different folds can also add a decorative touch to your tables and, depending on who is providing them, can be done ahead of time if you are DIYing your cutlery, by wrapping your silverware in your napkins ahead of the wedding day for a quick and easy setup.

Here are a few popular ways to place set your tables for guests.

1. BASIC TABLE SETTING. This includes a fork, knife, and spoon, as well as one dinner plate. The napkin can be folded and placed on the plate with silverware on top of it, or you can have the napkin on top of the plate with the forks on the left of the plate and the knife and spoons on the right side of the plate.

2. INFORMAL DINNER SETTING. Keep the aspects of the basic table setting (above) and add a salad plate and salad fork, along with bread and butter plates at the top left of your dinner plate. You can also add wine and water glasses to this setup.

3. FORMAL DINNER SETTING. Start with the layout of the informal dinner setting (above) and then add two wine glasses, one for a white wine and one for the red wine. You can also add a charger underneath the dinner plate and incorporate a coffee cup for the dessert portion of the meal.

CHAPTER 7

THE LAST 30 DAYS
& HAPPILY EVER AFTER

Congratulations! You are in the final stretch of your wedding day. Within the last 30 days, you can see the light at the end of the tunnel. As you get closer and closer to your wedding day, speak with your wedding planner, whether they have been working with you the entire length of your engagement or are just entering the picture to assist for the big day, to discuss and review your day-of schedule and your vendor lists, and to start confirming that all vendors have been paid in full.

During the last 30 days of your engagement, any final loose ties will need to be addressed, RSVPs must be confirmed, and guest counts should be reported to your caterer and venue to ensure you have enough food and space for all of your guests.

Before you become too overwhelmed, though, take a deep breath! You are so close to the big day, and you have so many people and vendors who are excited to make your day amazing.

A FINALIZED CHECKLIST OF EVERYTHING THAT NEEDS TO BE DONE

Being less than 45 days out from the wedding, you should be wrapping up plans and allowing yourself time to relax before the big day. This all starts with proper preparation and keeping everything organized.

You will need to have a schedule for the rehearsal dinner/ceremony day and a schedule for the wedding day.

Talk with your wedding planner about how you will arrange your wedding day and start filling in your plans on how you want your day to look.

REHEARSAL DAY SCHEDULE

TIME	ACTIVITY	WHO'S NEEDED
11:00 A.M.–11:30 A.M.		
11:30 A.M.–12:00 P.M.		
12:00 P.M.–12:30 P.M.		
12:30 P.M.–1:00 P.M.		
1:00 P.M.–1:30 P.M.		
1:30 P.M.–2:00 P.M.		
2:00 P.M.–2:30 P.M.		
2:30 P.M.–3:00 P.M.		
3:00 P.M.–3:30 P.M.		
3:30 P.M.–4:00 P.M.		
4:00 P.M.–4:30 P.M.		
4:30 P.M.–5:00 P.M.		
5:00 P.M.–5:30 P.M.		

Time	Activity	Who's Needed
5:30 P.M.–6:00 P.M.		
6:00 P.M.–6:30 P.M.		
6:30 P.M.–7:00 P.M.		
7:00 P.M.–7:30 P.M.		
7:30 P.M.–8:00 P.M.		
8:00 P.M.–8:30 P.M.		
8:30 P.M.–9:00 P.M.		
9:00 P.M.–9:30 P.M.		
9:30 P.M.–10:00 P.M.		

WEDDING DAY SCHEDULE

Time	Activity	Who's Needed
7:30 A.M.–8:00 A.M.		
8:00 A.M.–8:30 A.M.		
8:30 A.M.–9:00 A.M.		
9:00 A.M.–9:30 A.M.		
9:30 A.M.–10:00 A.M.		
10:00 A.M.–10:30 A.M.		
10:30 A.M.–11:00 A.M.		
11:00 A.M.–11:30 A.M.		
11:30 A.M.–12:00 P.M.		
12:00 P.M.–12:30 P.M.		
12:30 P.M.–1:00 P.M.		
1:00 P.M.–1:30 P.M.		

TIME	ACTIVITY	WHO'S NEEDED
1:30 P.M.–2:00 P.M.		
2:00 P.M.–2:30 P.M.		
2:30 P.M.–3:00 P.M.		
3:00 P.M.–3:30 P.M.		
3:30 P.M.–4:00 P.M.		
4:00 P.M.–4:30 P.M.		
4:30 P.M.–5:00 P.M.		
5:00 P.M.–5:30 P.M.		
5:30 P.M.–6:00 P.M.		
6:00 P.M.–6:30 P.M.		
6:30 P.M.–7:00 P.M.		
7:00 P.M.–7:30 P.M.		
7:30 P.M.–8:00 P.M.		
8:00 P.M.–8:30 P.M.		
8:30 P.M.–9:00 P.M.		
9:00 P.M.–9:30 P.M.		
9:30 P.M.–10:00 P.M.		
10:00 P.M.–10:30 P.M.		
10:30 P.M.–11:00 P.M.		
11:00 P.M.–11:30 P.M.		
11:30 P.M.–12:00 A.M.		

Confirming with Vendors

Have your wedding planner send out confirmation emails at least 14 days before the wedding to all of your vendors to ensure that they have the correct information and are updated with any changes to your day-of schedule. This gives everyone enough time to update his/her information and plan for your big day.

A NOTE OF ADVICE: Brides, please, you need to rest! Have someone else do this. Here is a quick template your Maid of Honor, Wedding Planner, or parent can use to send out to your vendors:

> Hi!
>
> I want to confirm your arrival time of _____p.m. for my wedding
> at [*Wedding Venue*] in [*City, State*]. The address is [*insert address*],
> and you can park [*insert where they can park*] when you arrive.
> All vendors must be off the venue premises by _____p.m.
> Let me know if you have any questions!
>
> Thanks,
>
> _____

Below is a chart you can hand off to someone the day of your wedding to ensure that all of your vendors have been contacted, confirmed, and arrived on your big day.

Vendor Type	Vendor Contact Name	Vendor Company	Vendor Phone
COORDINATOR			
BAKER			
CATERER			
DJ/BAND			
OFFICIANT			
BARTENDING			
STAFFING SERVICE			
PHOTO BOOTH			
FLORIST			
PHOTOGRAPHER			
VIDEOGRAPHER			
VENUE			
CEREMONY MUSICIANS			
OTHER			

Vendor Email	Vendor Arrival Time	Vendor Departure Time	Emailed to Confirm?	Sent Schedule?

177

RSVP Cards & Food Requests

RSVPs should be received at least 45 days before the wedding, (or earlier depending on your caterers preference) to account for all food preferences. If you have not heard from certain guests, call them to confirm if they will be in attendance. Delegate this task to family members.

Refer to your RSVP list to keep track and confirm how many and which guests have RSVP'd for specific types of food. Copy the list and give it to your caterer and wedding planner, along with your seating chart if you are having a seated, plated dinner.

Processional & Recessional Order with Songs

Refer back to chapter 5 to look at your ideas for how and when you want people to walk down and back up the aisle during the ceremony.

If you have live music, you must send the list of songs you are requesting to your vendor at minimum 45 days before your wedding day (or earlier depending on your contract) to ensure that they will have enough time to rehearse and add songs to their repertoire.

TO TIP OR NOT TO TIP . . . YOUR VENDORS

Knowing whether or not to tip your vendors can be difficult for couples. While it is not mandatory, if you have room in your budget, you can give a small thank-you to your vendors.

Here are the recommended tips for each type of vendor.

CATERING: If your contract does not already include a gratuity fee, then 15 to 20 percent of your total bill is appropriate.

FLORIST: Once services are rendered, you can give a tip of 10 to 15 percent of your contract value.

WEDDING PLANNER: Planners do not expect tips; however, if yours did an incredible job or saved you huge amounts of money, you can tip between 10 and 15 percent as a way to say thank you.

PHOTOGRAPHER/VIDEOGRAPHER: Typically, tipping $50 to $100 per shooter is appropriate.

CEREMONY AND RECEPTION STAFF: $20 to $40 per person is an appropriate gesture to vendors in this category.

OFFICIANT: Most often, officiants will not be able to receive tips, but you can make a $100 donation to their assigned church as a thank-you. If your officiant did your wedding free of charge, it is often a kind gesture to thank them with a $50 to $100 tip.

HAIR AND MAKEUP ARTIST: Just as you would at a salon, offering a 15 to 20 percent is optional.

BAND OR DJ: Give $25 to $50 per band member, or a 10 percent tip of your contract value.

TRANSPORTATION: A 15 percent tip, if not included in your contract, is optional.

SOMETHING TO NOTE: While tips are wonderful, if you are unable to give them, it is 100 percent A-OK. As stated earlier, it is not mandatory to tip your wedding vendors. In fact, writing a stellar review or referring clients to your vendors are gestures that can actually go a lot further than a cash tip!

WHAT TO DO AFTER THE WEDDING
(ONLY READ THIS AFTER THE HONEYMOON—YOU DESERVE SOME REST!)

HOORAY! You made it! You are officially married!!! You survived wedding planning and looked superfine doing it. There are few things more stressful than planning a wedding, and you were able to conquer it like a champ!

Even though the wedding day is over, you are in for a treat now that you are married. Marriage is wonderful, beautiful, and challenging all at the same time, so get ready for a wild and crazy fun ride.

While you are adjusting to life as a married couple, here are a couple of things to consider as you are finishing up post-wedding items.

WRITE THANK-YOUS TO GUESTS

Now that you are officially wedded, it is time to get those thank-yous sent out. Since you kept such great care of tracking who gave you what at each event (refer back to your gift chart on page 32), you can easily see which gifts have not yet been acknowledged.

Handwritten notes are always more personal than typed, mass-produced letters, so to help you stay sincere while also saving time, here are three thank-you templates that you can rotate through as you work on getting those notes sent out!

THANK YOU TEMPLATES:

Template 1:

Dear _____,

Thank you so much for the _____. It was wonderful to see you at (the wedding/the bridal shower/etc.). Thank you for sharing such a special day with me. I can't wait to see you again soon!

        Best,

        _____

Template 2:

Dear _____,

Thank you for coming to the _____, we loved
seeing you there! Also, thank you for the _____.
We will be using it at the house a lot this upcoming year and will think
of you and your family when we do. Hope everyone is doing well.

Sincerely,

_____

Template 3:

Dear_____,

We are so thankful for you and your family! Your gift was just
what we needed, so thank you so much! We loved having you at
the wedding and look forward to catching up again soon.

Many Thanks,

_____

PRESERVE YOUR DRESS

Whether you rented or bought your wedding dress will determine what you will do with it after the wedding. If you don't need to return it to a designer shop or rental company, take your dress to a dry cleaner or bridal store and have it preserved.

Preserving your dress prevents future fabric damage, allowing you to save your dress for a future child's wedding. Alternatively, in the event you want to sell it in the future, you can!

If you would rather not preserve your wedding dress, the following page has five creative ideas for what you can do with it afterward!

5 CREATIVE
POST-WEDDING DRESS IDEAS

1. Donate it.
   - Brides Across America or Nearly Newlywed are sites that allow you donate your dress to military women and first responders.

2. Have an underwater photo session.
   - Get a photographer, find a lake or pool, and live out your dreams of becoming a mermaid!

3. Display it.
   - You can have your dress preserved and purchase a large shadow box to showcase your veil, pressed flowers from your bouquet, and a photo of you in your dress to decorate your home with a sentimental art gallery!

4. Transform it into something new!
   - If you don't plan on using your dress or saving it for future use, you can take it to a seamstress to transform it into a cocktail dress, or use the fabric for something completely new! Brides have created purses, wallets, and even quilt patches from their wedding dresses!

5. Have a paint photo shoot.
   - A white dress + bright colors = a fun photo shoot. Whether you want to play paintball or pop paint balloons with your boo, create a colorful experience that you will remember for years to come!

Change Your Name (if You Want!)

In the event you want to change your name after you get married, there are numerous things to think about. You may not even realize how many items you have that are under your maiden name!

Typically, in order to change your name, most states require your marriage license to prove that you did have a wedding, your driver's license and Social Security card, and sometimes even a birth certificate! You can check with the same office that you received your marriage license from or visit your state government's website to find the state and county regulations.

There are also websites that seem like they do all of the legal paper-work for you to change your name, but be careful! Some websites only organize your paperwork, leaving you to go in person to each office and change your bank accounts, social media accounts, and so on.

To change your name, the easiest thing is to follow the simple steps below to get your paperwork in order, and then take the name change process one step at a time!

1. GET YOUR MARRIAGE LICENSE.

- Most states require that you send in the marriage license within 30 days of your wedding so that they can file it in your county. They will then send back your original certificate once it is scanned and saved in their archives.

2. CHANGE YOUR SOCIAL SECURITY CARD.

- In order to change many other documents, you will need to have a valid Social Security card, so do this step first. Look at your county clerk's website to see if they have downloadable paperwork you can fill out at home and bring into the office.

3. GO TO THE MOTOR VEHICLE DEPARTMENT.

- With your updated Social Security card, marriage license, name change form (typically), and a small fee, you can update your driver's license in all states.

4. UPDATE YOUR BANK ACCOUNTS.

- Bring your updated driver's license and Social Security card to update your checking and savings accounts. Your banks will then send you updated credit and debit cards based on the type of account you have with them.

5. START CHECKING OFF THE LIST BELOW.

- Credit cards
- Employer's payroll, benefits, and insurance
- Social media accounts
- Car insurance
- Financial investment portfolios
- Electric and utility providers
- Doctors' offices
- Post office (especially if you moved to a new address after getting married!)
- Voter registration office
- Airline and rewards programs (claim all of your miles!)
- Passport office

On the following page is an area where you can check off whether you currently have any paperwork, credit cards, house payments, car payments, financial accounts, passports, and so on that will need to be notified once you officially change your name.

TYPE OF ACCOUNT	HAVE YOU CHANGED IT?	DATE YOU UPDATED INFORMATION
CREDIT CARDS		
EMPLOYER'S PAYROLL, BENEFITS, AND INSURANCE		
INSURANCE (CAR, HOME, LIFE)		
SOCIAL MEDIA ACCOUNTS		
ATTORNEY		
FINANCIAL INVESTMENT PORTFOLIOS		
ELECTRIC AND UTILITY PROVIDERS		
DOCTORS' OFFICES		
POST OFFICE		
VOTER REGISTRATION OFFICE		
AIRLINE AND REWARDS PROGRAMS		
PASSPORT OFFICE		

If you want to hyphenate your name, the process is fairly similar. A county clerk must approve any change to your original name, and sometimes you must fill out a name-change petition for the court.

Call your county clerk (the same place you received your marriage license) and ask if they have a specific process for your name change.

Lastly, if you don't want to change your name, no problem! You keep doing you, you beautiful bride, and live happily ever after with your new spouse!

WRITE REVIEWS FOR YOUR VENDORS

Writing reviews for your vendors is an amazing way to share some love with the people who served you and your boo on your wedding day.

If you worked with a vendor that you absolutely loved, then make sure the world knows about it! You can write reviews online, or you can send a review by email that the vendor can later share with other brides who want to know about the experiences brides have had.

To write a good review for your vendors, you don't need to write a novel. A couple of sentences, detailing the vendor's communication and quality of service, as well as a possible personal moment that you might have shared with that particular vendor.

Here's an example of a great review!

> [*Insert name*] was an amazing [*insert wedding vendor type*]. We loved how easy and effortlessly we could communicate with them via email, text, or phone. After our wedding, we even grabbed dinner together! It was so wonderful to work together and catch up after the wedding.

Here's a checklist for you to mark off once you have written a review for each of your vendors!

VENDOR TYPE	DID YOU WRITE A REVIEW?

SHARE/POST PHOTOS ONLINE & TAG YOUR FRIENDS!

You know that your friends want to see your wedding photos just as much as you do, so don't be shy! Once you get your wedding album, let friends and family know, and if you end up posting them on social media, make sure to tag your friends to remind them of the best day ever! You can reuse your wedding hashtag to help guests and family track photos on sites like Instagram or Pinterest.

You can even print out your favorite photos and tape or glue them inside in this book as a keepsake that you can pass on to your children and grandchildren.

FILL THIS SPACE WITH ANY EXTRA NOTES YOU MAY HAVE:

_____

_____

_____

_____

_____

_____

_____

_____

_____

_____

_____

_____

_____

_____

_____

_____

_____

_____

LIVING HAPPILY EVER AFTER

As you reminisce about your wedding day, remember the sentimental and the funny moments that made your wedding day so uniquely yours.

While planning a wedding can be challenging and exciting, nothing is more amazing than seeing a marriage flourish, so best of luck to you, Mrs.! You are going to be an amazing spouse and cherish each season of life, from your engagement to when you're old and gray—you are worthy and dearly loved. Congrats to you and thank you for using this planner to help guide you throughout the wedding planning process.

xoxo,

KARA WEAVER

KARA WEAVER is a Texas born graduate of The University of Texas at Austin Red McCombs School of Business. She spent two years working in the corporate world, while also managing a growing side-hustle. Kara left her corporate job in the summer of 2018 to run her wedding planning business, Weddings By Weaver. When she's not working, you can find Kara snuggled up next to her husband, Jacob, binge watching Netlfix with a margarita in one hand, and a puppy paw in the other.

To connect, you can find her on social media platforms as @WeddingsbyWeaver or her website www.weddingsbyweaver.com.